★ A Guide to ★
Bicycling in Texas
TOURS, TIPS, AND MORE

GEORGE SEVRA

Lone Star Books
A Division of Gulf Publishing Company
Houston, Texas

Bicycling in Texas

Library of Congress Cataloging in Publication Data

Sevra, George.
    Bicycling in Texas.

    Includes index.
    1. Bicycle touring—Texas—Guide-books. 2. Texas—Description and travel—1981–
    —Guide-books.
    I. Title.

GV1045.5.T4S48   1985   917.64   85-6935
ISBN 0-88415-079-8

Enjoy the best of Texas with these Lone Star books:

The Alamo and Other Texas Missions to Remember
Amazing Texas Monuments and Museums
Backroads of Texas
Beachcomber's Guide to Gulf Coast Marine Life
The Best of Texas Festivals
Bicycling in Texas
Camper's Guide to Texas Parks, Lakes, and Forests/2nd Edition
From Texas Kitchens
Great Hometown Restaurants of Texas
A Guide to Fishing in Texas
A Guide to Historic Texas Inns and Hotels/2nd Edition
A Guide to Hunting in Texas
A Guide to Texas Lakes
A Guide to Texas Rivers and Streams
Hiking and Backpacking Trails of Texas/2nd Edition
A Line on Texas
Rock Hunting in Texas
Texas Birds: Where They Are and How to Find Them
Texas—Family Style
Traveling Texas Borders
Unsung Heroes of Texas
Why Stop? A Guide to Texas Roadside Historical Markers/2nd Edition

Special thanks to the Texas Department of Highways and Public Transportation for supplying the county maps contained in this book.

Contents

Introduction, v
Description of Terms, vii

Section 1: Area Tours, 1
Navasota, 3

    Where to Stay, 3

    What to See, 3

    City Tour, 6

    Tour #1: Washington-on-the-Brazos State Park, 7

    Tour #2: Washington-on-the-Brazos and Millican Loop, 8

    Tour #3: Anderson—Short Route, 9

    Tour #4: Anderson—FM 3090 Complete, 10

    Tour #5: Anderson—The Long Way, 12

    Tour #6: Plantersville - Magnolia, 13

Nacogdoches, 15

    Where to Stay, 15

    What to See, 15

    City Tour, 19

    Tour #1: Looneyville - Douglass, 20

    Tour #2: Shady Grove, 21

    Tour #3: Martinsville - Chireno, 22

    Tour #4: San Augustine, 23

Jefferson, 25

    Where to Stay, 25

    What to See, 28

    City Tour, 28

    Tour #1: Lodi - Mill Creek, 29

    Tour #2: Caddo Lake State Park, 30

    Tour #3: Lake O' The Pines Dam, 31

    Tour #4: Around Lake O' The Pines, 32

Kerrville/Fredericksburg, 33
    Where to Stay and Eat, 33
    What to See, 33
    City Tours, 36
    Tour #1: Kerrville State Park - Turtle Creek, 37
    Tour #2: Cedar Creek - Camp Verde, 38
    Tour #3: Fredericksburg - Harper, 40
    Tour #4: Lower Crabapple Road, 42
Burnet, 44
    Where to Stay, 44
    What to See, 44
    City Tour, 46
    Tour #1: Lake Victor, 47
    Tour #2: Longhorn Caverns State Park, 48
    Tour #3: Shady Grove Road - Bertram, 49
    Tour #4: Marble Falls - "The Notch," 50

Section 2: Spot Tours, 53

Kountze/Big Thicket, 55
Glen Rose, 59
Spur, 64
Palo Duro Canyon State Park, 67
Buffalo Lake National Wildlife Refuge, 70
Fort Davis, 73
Leakey, 77

Section 3: Intercity Tours, 81

Dallas to Houston, 83
Houston to Austin, 85
Austin to Dallas, 87
Austin to Corpus Christi, 89
San Antonio to Rio Grande Valley, 91
Appendix: Sources of Information, 93
    Chambers of Commerce, 93
    Map Sources, 94
    Bicycle Shops, 94

Index, 95

Introduction

The statement has been made countless times by people who don't know Texas (and even cyclists who should know better) that Texas is "flat and empty." This gross generalization can be made about many states and is certainly true of some parts of Texas, but there are other parts of Texas that offer the adventurous cyclist a wealth of riding and exploring.

This guide is intended to introduce you to the surprising wonders of bicycling in Texas. It is a sampler designed to give both general information about an area and several specific routes in the area for the cyclist to choose from. Sources of information are also supplied to enable you to create your own tour. From deep within the pine forests of East Texas to the heart-pounding mountains of West Texas to the not-as-flat-as-you-might-think Panhandle to the dense jungle-like Big Thicket, bicycling in Texas is a challenging and rewarding experience awaiting every level of cyclist willing to seek his or her limits.

The tours outlined in this book are divided into three categories: area tours, spot tours, and intercity routes. The area tours comprise three to five loop tours originating from one of six small towns with historic and scenic interest (Jefferson, Nacogdoches, Navasota, Burnet, Kerrville, and Fredericksburg).

The key word is "loop." Each tour incorporates a maximum of small-road cycling with a minimum of duplication. There are no out-and-back-on-the-same-road tours in this section.

Spot tours are single tours in one spot. These are the *best* tours in a particularly interesting region where area tours would be impractical. Each of these tours will vividly immerse the cyclist in the sublime beauty and breathtaking splendor of the area.

The intercity routes connect major cities in Central and South Texas. (The cities in West Texas and the Panhandle region require arduous journeys that should only be attempted by the fittest of experienced cyclists.) The intercity routes offer an alternative to riding

CANYON
PALO DURO
CANYON
STATE PARK
BUFFALO
LAKE
NATIONAL
WILDLIFE
REFUGE

SPUR

DALLAS

JEFFERSON

GLEN ROSE

NACOGDOCHES

BURNET

KOUNTZE/BIG THICKET

NAVASOTA

FORT DAVIS/DAVIS MOUNTAINS

FREDERICKSBURG

AUSTIN

KERRVILLE

HOUSTON

LEAKEY

SAN ANTONIO

CORPUS CHRISTI

BROWNSVILLE

The bicycle tours in this book originate from the cities indicated on this map.

along the access road of an interstate highway. Wherever possible the least-traveled roads were chosen, although in some cases (e.g., around Houston) this was impossible.

All the tours described in this guide are not the only tours in the area. They are intended to give you some place to start and to act as a base from which to create other tours. Nor is each route described in the minutest detail so that some things are left for you to discover on your trip.

There are no time limits set on any tours in this book. Touring means visiting a place to see what is there. You cannot tour at 20 mph. "Miles-per-hour" is totally irrelevant when touring. So instead of "allow 4 hours," why not allow all day? The quality of the ride is more important than the speed.

A Guide to Bicycling in Texas will expand your cycling horizons beyond your expectations, because Texas is a diverse and wonderous state to explore on a bicycle. Try it! The rewards of discovery are worth the endeavor.

Description of Terms

To add a bit of flavor to the descriptions of the tours, a few new terms have been coined. As your cycling experience grows, you will no doubt coin a few choice terms of your own.

Huff-n-puff—This is a steep uphill, usually long, that requires granny gears and screaming thighs. It is unmerciful going up, but a proud accomplishment when you reach the top. (Note: Always take a moment to look behind you at the vista that has unveiled. You have earned the view.)

Whoosh—This is the opposite of a huff-n-puff. It is a steep downhill, usually much too short, that requires nerves of aluminum alloy and good brakes. (Note: Watch for gravel, hairpin curves, and loose livestock!)

Whoop-dee-doos—This is a series of short, low, rolling dips that don't require a gear change. Your downhill momentum can usually carry you over the ups.

The following legend should be used in conjunction with the county maps on pages 4–5, 16–17, 26–27, 34–35, 45, 56–57, 60-61, 65, 68, 71, 74–78.

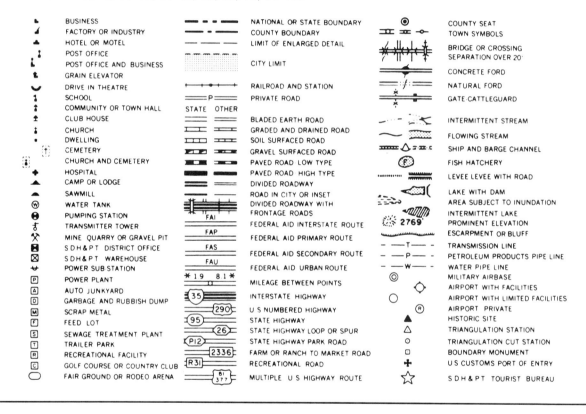

BUSINESS	NATIONAL OR STATE BOUNDARY	COUNTY SEAT
FACTORY OR INDUSTRY	COUNTY BOUNDARY	TOWN SYMBOLS
HOTEL OR MOTEL	LIMIT OF ENLARGED DETAIL	BRIDGE OR CROSSING SEPARATION OVER 20'
POST OFFICE		
POST OFFICE AND BUSINESS	CITY LIMIT	CONCRETE FORD
GRAIN ELEVATOR		NATURAL FORD
DRIVE IN THEATRE	RAILROAD AND STATION	GATE CATTLEGUARD
SCHOOL	PRIVATE ROAD	
COMMUNITY OR TOWN HALL	STATE OTHER	
CLUB HOUSE	BLADED EARTH ROAD	INTERMITTENT STREAM
CHURCH	GRADED AND DRAINED ROAD	FLOWING STREAM
DWELLING	SOIL SURFACED ROAD	SHIP AND BARGE CHANNEL
CEMETERY	GRAVEL SURFACED ROAD	FISH HATCHERY
CHURCH AND CEMETERY	PAVED ROAD LOW TYPE	LEVEE LEVEE WITH ROAD
HOSPITAL	PAVED ROAD HIGH TYPE	LAKE WITH DAM
CAMP OR LODGE	DIVIDED ROADWAY	AREA SUBJECT TO INUNDATION
SAWMILL	ROAD IN CITY OR INSET	INTERMITTENT LAKE
WATER TANK	DIVIDED ROADWAY WITH FRONTAGE ROADS	PROMINENT ELEVATION
PUMPING STATION	FAI	ESCARPMENT OR BLUFF
TRANSMITTER TOWER	FEDERAL AID INTERSTATE ROUTE	TRANSMISSION LINE
MINE QUARRY OR GRAVEL PIT	FAP	PETROLEUM PRODUCTS PIPE LINE
SDH&PT DISTRICT OFFICE	FEDERAL AID PRIMARY ROUTE	WATER PIPE LINE
SDH&PT WAREHOUSE	FAS	MILITARY AIRBASE
POWER SUB STATION	FEDERAL AID SECONDARY ROUTE	AIRPORT WITH FACILITIES
POWER PLANT	FAU	AIRPORT WITH LIMITED FACILITIES
AUTO JUNKYARD	FEDERAL AID URBAN ROUTE	AIRPORT PRIVATE
GARBAGE AND RUBBISH DUMP	MILEAGE BETWEEN POINTS	HISTORIC SITE
SCRAP METAL	INTERSTATE HIGHWAY	TRIANGULATION STATION
FEED LOT	U S NUMBERED HIGHWAY	TRIANGULATION CUT STATION
SEWAGE TREATMENT PLANT	STATE HIGHWAY	BOUNDARY MONUMENT
TRAILER PARK	STATE HIGHWAY LOOP OR SPUR	U S CUSTOMS PORT OF ENTRY
RECREATIONAL FACILITY	STATE HIGHWAY PARK ROAD	SDH&PT TOURIST BUREAU
GOLF COURSE OR COUNTRY CLUB	FARM OR RANCH TO MARKET ROAD	
FAIR GROUND OR RODEO ARENA	RECREATIONAL ROAD	
	MULTIPLE U S HIGHWAY ROUTE	

Section 1
Area Tours

Navasota

Where to Stay

CAMPING

Grassy Creek Mobile Home Park
P.O. Box 668
Navasota, TX 77868
(409) 825-6883 or 825-6245

Located 4.5 miles south of downtown Navasota on TX 6. Tent camping is $2 per night with showers; $3 per night with electricity. Mrs. T. S. Falkenbury, proprietress.

MOTELS

Vanguard Inn
711 N. LaSalle St.
(Business Rte. 6N)
Navasota, TX 77868

Located just three blocks north of the town center. Bikes are permitted in the rooms.

Another motel is the Hammett Motel, located three miles south of town on TX 6 Business.

What to See

LA SALLE STATUE

This monument honors René Robert Cavelier, Sieur de la Salle, who was murdered by his own men along the Brazos River in March 1687. It is officially recognized by the French Government.

NAVASOTA STRAND

This is a one-block restored section of Railroad Street, built in the 1860s and 1870s. It includes the Giesel House (ca. 1860) and the P.A. Smith Hotel (ca. 1876).

MAIN STREET WALKING TOUR

A brochure is available at the chamber of commerce that describes the Historic Commercial District of Navasota. Cotton was "king" at the turn of the century, and this is reflected in the many buildings on this short tour. Don't forget to look at the sides and backs of these buildings, most of which are original construction. There are 41 points of interest described in this tour brochure. The tour covers about one mile.

EAST WASHINGTON STREET

With its many homes dating from the Victorian era.

HOLLAND STREET

Numerous old churches and homes display the beauty of the Victorian era, when only one or two homes were built to a city block.

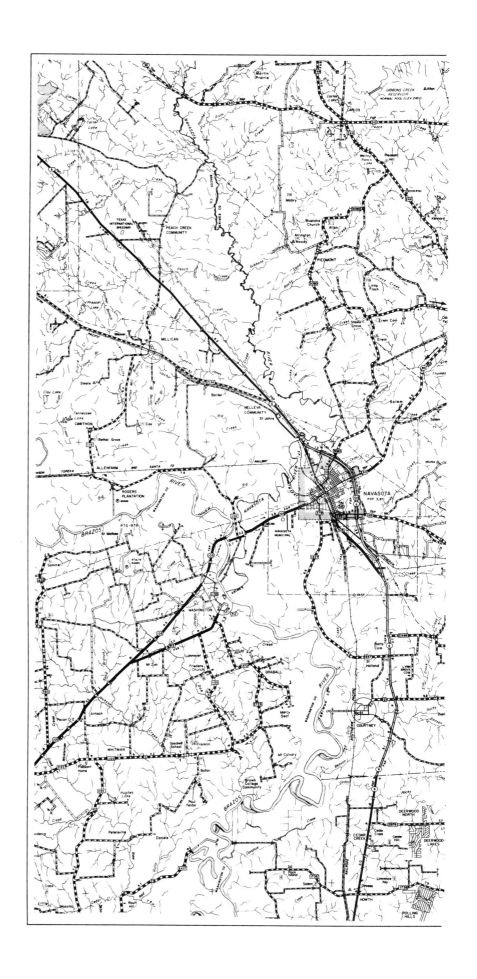

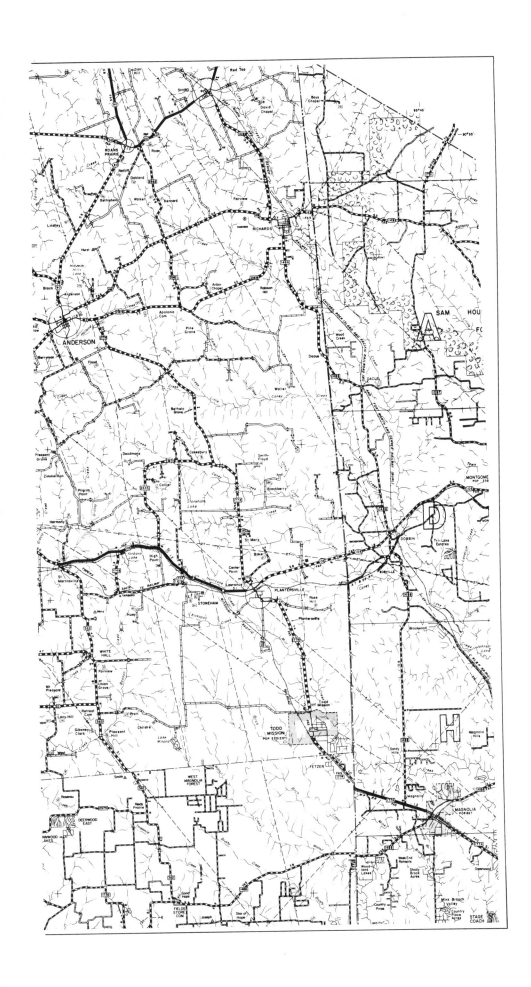

City Tour

The tour of Navasota includes a cycling portion of about five miles and a walking portion of one mile. A brochure with a map describing the walking tour is available at the chamber of commerce, a bright, blue building located one block south of the stoplight on South La Salle (TX 6 Bus.) at McAlpine Street. The cycling portion will also begin here. Parking is available at the chamber.

From the chamber of commerce, ride south on La Salle one block and turn left onto Holland. There are two historic churches and four historic homes along Holland Street, beginning with the first Presbyterian Church on your right. This church was organized in 1868. The present structure was built in 1894, and the fine masonry work on the building is typical of the era. One block further, also on the right, is the Lucas Home (ca. 1895). This white frame house originally had a widow's walk, but this was destroyed by Hurricane Alicia and replaced with the present turret. Across the intersection, still on the right, is the First Baptist Church. Organized in 1869, the present buildings were begun in 1890. At the end of this block on the right is the Craig House (ca. 1895). This house once possessed a round corner porch with cupola, but Hurricane Alicia coveted it as well.

Across the street past the intersection is the Steele House (ca. 1896). In the next block, on the right, is the Jesse Youens Home (ca. 1871). There is a carriage house converted to a garage on the Woods Street side of the house.

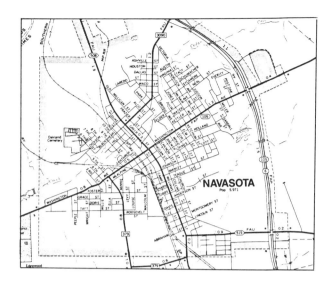

Turn right at the end of Holland onto Ketchum Street. Ride two blocks to the "T," and turn right again onto Lane Street. Ride two blocks to another "T," and turn left onto Leon Street. Then ride two blocks to the end of the road, and turn right onto Manley Street. Continue for two long blocks to St. Patrick's Catholic Church, then turn right onto Church Street. In this block, on the left, is the home of former Texas Lieutenant Governor George D. Neal, who purchased it in 1833 after retiring to Navasota to practice law.

Turn left at this intersection onto Johnson Street. The large red brick house on the right is the Emory Terrell home (ca. 1904), an exceptional example of the fruits of King Cotton. Ride two blocks to La Salle, turn right, and go to the stoplight. Turn right onto Washington Street where you are again presented with a lovely array of historic structures. One and one-half blocks from the stoplight, at the head of the median, is a statue honoring the French explorer, La Salle. Other places of special note include the Brooks-Ward House on the right at Woods Street and the Stewart-Davis House at the corner of Judson and Washington streets. Across from this house, down a small unpaved road (Castle Drive) is the Templeman-Grice House; also known as "The Castle."

Return on East Washington Street to the stoplight. Just past the light and on the left is the City Cafe. After a delicious meal, store your bike, and begin your walking tour from here. Refer to the brochure from the chamber of commerce for directions.

The buildings along Railroad Avenue are some of the oldest in the city and can be seen on a walking tour of downtown Navasota.

TOUR #1
Washington-on-the-Brazos State Park

ROUTE
TX 105 west - 6.2 miles
FM 1155 south - 1.4 miles
FM 912 west - .2 miles
Entrance to Washington-on-the-Brazos State Park
FM 912 west - .6 miles
FM 1370 south - 3.5 miles
FM 2726 west - 3.3 miles
FM 1155 north - 7.4 miles
TX 105 east - 6.2 miles

DISTANCE
28.8 miles/46.1 kilometers

TERRAIN
Flat

TRAFFIC
Light

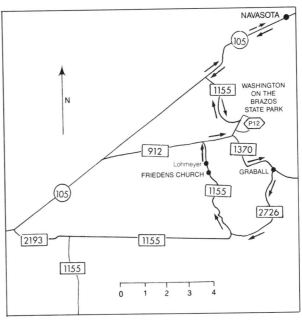

Heading west on TX 105, you immediately enter the rich, open farm lands for which this area is noted, where cotton and corn are the agricultural mainstays. At 3.6 miles, the road crosses the Navasota River, and about .2 mile past is a small road to the left, opposite FM 159. At the end of this road is the confluence of the Navasota and Brazos Rivers where LaSalle is said to have been shot by one of his own men.

Continuing on TX 105, crossing the Brazos River, it is 1.7 miles to the junction with FM 1155. At the junction, turn left and follow the signs to Washington. Washington served as capital of the Texas Republic from 1842 to 1845. The town thrived until the mid 1850s when the railroad passed it by. In Washington is the Kountry Kupboard Gift Shop and Restaurant, where you can buy nice gifts and excellent food. Just around the right-hand curve is Washington-on-the-Brazos State Park.

In the park is a replica of the building used at the signing of the Texas Declaration of Independence on March 2, 1836. According to archaeologists, the present Independence Hall is located on the same site as the original. Also in the park is Barrington, the home of Anson Jones, last president of the Texas Republic. The house was built about 1845 near its present location. Jones, despondent over numerous failures, sold Barrington in December 1857. Less than one month later, on January 9, 1858, he commited suicide in Houston. (For those who wish at this point to return to Navasota, retrace the route on FM 1155 and TX 105.)

From the park continue west on FM 1155 to FM 1370. The cemetery at this junction has many old and interesting markers for epitaph collectors. Turn south on FM 1370 and begin a wonderfully easy ride through farm lands west of the Brazos River. In the spring, this area is spectacular with fields of bluebonnets. After 3.5 miles, turn right on FM 2726. Follow it to FM 1155 and turn right (north). About 2 miles from this junction is a bridge across Doe Run Creek, which is a typical example of the numerous feeder creeks of the Brazos River. Continuing 2.5 miles to FM 912, turn right on FM 1155. From here retrace the route to Navasota on which you came out. It's about 9 miles back to town.

TOUR #2
Washington-on-the-Brazos and Millican Loop

ROUTE
TX 105 west - 6.2 miles
FM 1155 south - 1.4 miles
Entrance to Washington-on-
the-Brazos State Park
Park Road P12 - .3 miles
FM 1155 north - 1.4 miles
TX 105 east - 2.4 miles
FM 159 north - 13.9 miles
FM 2154 south - 5.1 miles
TX 6 south - 4.3 miles

DISTANCE
35 miles/56 kilometers

TERRAIN
Flat with short rolling section

TRAFFIC
Light to nil

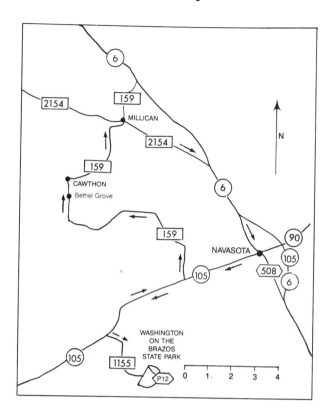

See Tour #1 for the route description to Washington-on-the-Brazos State Park. Retrace the route on FM 1155 to TX 105. On TX 105, cross the Brazos River and turn left on FM 159 (north).

FM 159 winds over flat bottomland through several farm co-op communities that are excellent examples of large-scale farming. For the last 4 or so miles the road dips and rolls through dense pine forests interspersed with stands of oak, cottonwood, and elm to the town of Millican. Located at the junction of FM 159 and FM 2154, Millican has only a small store (open seven days) and a post office—in a portable building, no less!

Millican is named after Andrew Millican, the first white settler in Grimes County. In 1820 Millican built a log cabin on Ten Mile Creek. He sold his land to the second white settler in the county and disappeared into history.

Turning right at the junction, the road gets flat again and stays that way to the edge of Navasota, where a small uphill provides a lovely view to the east and north.

The Craig house, built about 1895, can be seen on the Navasota city tour.

TOUR #3
Anderson—Short Route

ROUTE
TX 6 Bus. north - .1 mile
FM 3090 north - 7.9 miles
FM 149 east - 4.5 miles
TX 90 south - 9.7 miles

DISTANCE
22.2 miles/35.5 kilometers

TERRAIN
Gently rolling

TRAFFIC
Light to nil

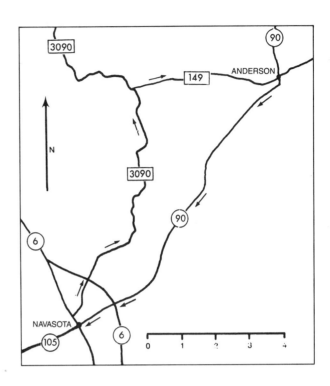

The most charming road in the area has to be FM 3090. Once past the TX 6 overpass, you climb to a rewarding view of the surrounding area. This is dairy farm country. Grimes County is called "The Land of Milk and Honey" because of the many excellent dairies. About 2 miles from the overpass are three small bridges close together. The third bridge crosses Holland Creek, named for Frances Holland, who came to Texas in 1822. One of her sons, Tapley Holland, died at the Alamo. It is reported that Tapley was the first to cross the line drawn by Col. Travis, saying, "Let me be the first to give a life for Texas."

This peaceful little road continues to a "T" intersection with FM 149 turning right and FM 3090 continuing left. Tour #4 turns left here.

Tour #3 turns right on FM 149 and rolls for 4.5 pleasant miles into Anderson.

Anderson is the county seat for Grimes County. It possesses a unique Victorian-style courthouse. Built in 1891 of hand-molded brick and native stone trim, it was the site of the trial of a Clyde Barrow gang member. When the verdict of guilty was rendered, he exclaimed that he would meet the court members again in a "warmer place." There are a total of 28 historic places described in the newspaper brochure titled, "Historic Grimes County and An-derson Texas," written by Julie Caddel, chairperson of The Grimes County Historical Commission. It is available at the Navasota Chamber of Commerce. The tour is an easy walk from the courthouse and includes the Bay Food Store. Built about 1860, it is the oldest commercial building in Anderson. Also see the Fantrop Inn (ca. 1834), which became the location of a stage stop on the route from Houston to Huntsville. Take the time for this tour. It's well worthwhile.

Taking TX 90 south from Anderson, you will again cross Holland Creek (the third bridge about 3.5 miles from town). TX 90 is a nice, wide open road with plenty of smooth shoulder. About 1.5 miles from Navasota, on the left, is a small, stone ruin. Just beyond, on the same side, is a white frame house. The stone ruins are the remnants of Foster Gin, which ceased operation in 1930, another victim of the Great Depression. The frame house was built by Ira Camp for his daughter and was purchased in 1833 by R.B.S. Foster, whose descendants still have ownership.

TX 90 into Navasota is also East Washington Street, where you can take another look at the stately homes along its way.

TOUR #4
Anderson—FM 3090 Complete

ROUTE
TX 6 Bus. north - .1 mile
FM 3090 north - 17.8 miles
FM 244 south - 5.7 miles
TX 90 south - 11.1 miles

DISTANCE
34.7 miles/55.5 kilometers

TERRAIN
Gently rolling

TRAFFIC
Light to nil

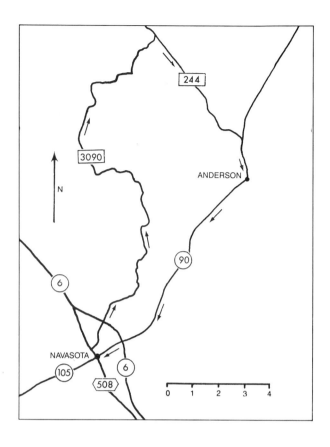

This tour is perhaps the most complete for the area. Encompassing as it does, the best road and historic Anderson, it gives the cyclist a real "feel" for the countryside and its past. See Tour #3 for the first section of this route.

Beginning at the "T" intersection of FM 3090 and FM 149, turn left and follow FM 3090. This entire road is a result of the Work Projects Administration. Some 4 miles past a "Load Zoned Bridge Ahead" sign is said bridge and a small bronze plaque that says, "Work Projects Administrations 1938–1940." The pylons on the left are from the original bridge. This bridge crosses Rocky Creek. Just a short distance further is another bridge, which crosses Sand Creek. The WPA only replaced the old pylons on this bridge. The underside of the bridge, constructed of lumber bolted together, is still original. Directly ahead is a marked curve to the right, and about 200 yards past this, on the left, is a small log cabin with a covered picnic area adjacent. Next to the aluminum gate is a historical marker for Piedmont Springs Resort. As early as 1850 the three sulphur springs at this site were host to a health spa and resort business. Follow the small sulphur creek past the old brick retaining wall and you will find the last evidence of a four-story hotel which boasted 100 rooms. Built in 1860, the Piedmont

Cycling on TX 90 toward Anderson on Tours #4 and #5 presents you with a great downhill plunge into town.

A map of a walking tour of Anderson (about a dozen blocks) is available at the courthouse. Take a long break and enjoy the tour.

Hotel entertained many notables of the era, including General Sam Houston. The Great Panic of 1870 closed the hotel forever, and these stone foundations are all that remain of its former glory.

The school house on the right as you leave Piedmont was built at the turn of the century and was used until the 1960s. The next 5 miles roll gently through beautiful farm and ranch country, which includes near the end of FM 3090 the Waltrip Ranch with its several miles of white, wooden fences.

FM 3090 ends at FM 244. Tour #5 turns left here. Tour #4 turns right. The road continues with gentle rises and curves. On the left, 4.8 miles from the junction is another historical marker. This is the site of a munitions factory operated by the Dance Brothers, where cannonballs destined to make life difficult for the Union Army were manufactured. After Appomattox, the cannonballs were melted down and used in construction, and nothing is left of the factory today.

Turning right onto TX 90, it is just a short jaunt until the Anderson Courthouse comes into view. On top of the next short hill, on the right, is the old Buffington House. Originally built in 1890, it was enlarged and remodeled in a Victorian style in 1903. To obtain the best view of its stately turretted grandeur, descend the hill until abreast the pond, stop and look back. Magnificent!

Complete the downhill and a short pedal up will bring you to the Anderson Courthouse. Park your bike in front and begin the walking tour as described in Tour #3. The remainder of Tour #4 is the same as the walking tour of Tour #3. Please refer to same.

TOUR #5
Anderson—The Long Way

ROUTE
TX 6 Bus. north - .1 mile
FM 3090 north - 17.8 miles
FM 244 north - 2.4 miles
TX 30 east - 9.1 miles
TX 90 south - 17.0 miles

DISTANCE
46.4 miles/74.7 kilometers

TERRAIN
Gently rolling

TRAFFIC
Light to nil

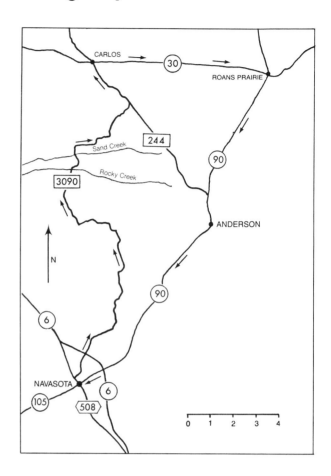

This tour is for those who wish to "stretch" their mileage but miss none of the sights of Tours #3 and #4.

Picking up at the junction of FM 3090 and FM 244 from Tour #4, turn left onto FM 244. The town of Carlos is 2.4 miles further at the junction of FM 244 and TX 30. The gas station/store on the opposite corner has a very good cafe, the perfect rest and snack stop to energize you for the 9 miles to Roan's Prairie. Take TX 30 east, and start pumping.

In Roan's Prairie, just past the junction of TX 30 and TX 90, turn right onto the dirt street opposite the "bargain center." The street has no name and will lead you to the Roan's Prairie Baptist Church where Lyndon Johnson's grandfather was pastor.

Returning to the junction, turn left (south) on TX 90 to Anderson. This section of the tour will have the biggest hills, but even they are not difficult. As with Tours #3 and #4, be sure to see all of Anderson. Follow TX 90 for the 9.7 miles back to Navasota.

The peaceful, quiet, gently rolling countryside on FM 3090 near Navasota (Tours #3 and #4) makes this section one of the most enjoyable to ride.

TOUR #6
Plantersville - Magnolia

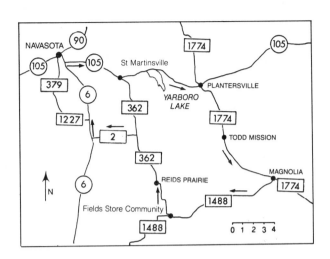

ROUTE
TX 105 east - 15.1 miles
FM 1774 south - 13.0 miles
FM 1488 east - 11.0 miles
FM 362 north - 9.0 miles
FM 2 west - 4.2 miles
TX 6 north - 1.8 miles
FM 1227 west - 8.8 miles
FM 379 north - 1.0 miles
TX 105 east - .5 miles

DISTANCE
64.4 miles/103.0 kilometers

TERRAIN
Flat to rolling

TRAFFIC
Light to nil

This tour encompasses all aspects of the varied terrain and scenery of the area—from the rolling forests to the flat bottomlands of the Navasota and Brazos Rivers.

Beginning in Navasota, TX 105 east is also East Washington Street with its stately, turn-of-the-century homes. Follow the signs to the right at the freeway (TX 6) and stay on the access road. About 1.4 miles later, turn left under the highway. Much of TX 105 is being enlarged to a four-lane divided highway with wide shoulders. There is no telling what conditions you will find along here for the next couple of years. However, the scenery is pretty, rolling ranch country.

At Plantersville, turn right onto FM 1774. On the right is the new store and on the left is the now-closed Greenwood General Merchandise built around 1880. It is such a loss for these historic places to fall to ruin.

Just after the railroad tracks, on the left, is the Plantersville Masonic Lodge, built before 1850. The lodge occupied the second floor, while the first floor served as the first school in

The Steele House (ca. 1896) is one of the many grand old homes you can see as you cycle around Navasota.

the area. The first meeting of the Methodist Church was here in 1853. A block further on the right is the Plantersville Baptist Church, where one of the original organizers in 1861 was George W. Baines, great-grandfather of Lyndon Baines Johnson. This building was built in 1872 at a cost of $2,700 in gold.

This section of the tour, FM 1774 from Plantersville to Magnolia, is part of the Dallas-to-Houston Intercity Route.

Navasota has several beautiful old homes including the Lucas house, built about 1890.

Once past Plantersville, the route enters gently rolling pine forests. The forest is close to the road and adds a true measure of intimacy to the ride. Six miles south on FM 1774 is the site of the Texas Renaissance Festival—a magnificent theme park dedicated to the joys and excesses of Medieval Europe in the thirteenth to sixteenth centuries. The festival is open in October and the first half of November, on weekends only and traffic will be heavy during this time. This is a must-see annual event, and camping is available on the grounds while the festival is open.

When you enter Magnolia, the route turns right and crosses the same railroad tracks you crossed in Plantersville. The flat road to the left is the continuation of the Dallas-Houston route. For the next 40-odd miles south to Houston, this road gets busier and more commercial.

Cycling out of Magnolia on FM 1488, the pine forest gets a little scruffier as it changes to live oaks and mesquite trees. The road remains gently rolling, but traffic becomes almost non-existent.

At the junction of FM 1488 and FM 362 north, a marker describes the Field Store Community. Sadly, like many other communities founded in the early-to-mid 1800s, nothing is left of the original town.

There is a rather incongruous modern horse barn to the right, just after turning onto FM 362. Also to the right is a small pond with an island, which forms a splendid, tranquil scene amidst the pines.

As the road gently rolls northward, about 4 miles from Magnolia, is Ried's Prairie First Baptist Church, built in 1895.

Retreat Community, at the junction of FM 362 and FM 2, is where George C. Childress wrote the Declaration of Independence for Texas prior to the signing at Washington-on-the-Brazos. Retreat also served as the capital of the Republic for four days, from March 18 to March 21, 1836.

Turning left (west) onto FM 2, this narrow, old road leads to more rolling terrain. The woods are sparse and the farms poorer. Fortunately, the traffic is virtually nil. After a quiet, pleasant rollercoaster ride on FM 2, the ride on TX 6 will be an unpleasant interruption. Turn north onto the shoulder of TX 6, and suffer only 1.8 miles of this expanse to the next junction.

The small, white frame St. Holland's Church on the opposite side of the highway, as well as the highway signs, marks the junction with FM 1227. This little church and cemetery are "new" (ca. 1920). FM 1227 reenters the bottomlands bordering the Brazos River. As you circle along this stretch, you may notice many fieldhands dressed in white coveralls along with uniformed men on horseback with each group. The two watertowers ahead of you belong to the Wallace Park Unit of the Texas Department of Corrections. When you ride past the main entrance to this minimum security prison, remember, the guards take their jobs seriously, and so should you.

Just when you guess you have reached the end and are about to enter Navasota, to the left before the junction of FM 1227 and FM 379, in one of the small fenced pens are several bison—a surprising finish to a very diverse ride. Continue straight on FM 379 into Navasota.

Nacogdoches

Where to Stay

CAMPING

Trailer Village Camper Park
US 59 (North Street)
(409) 564-0540

This is located near the Old North Church. Tent camping is permitted.

MOTELS

The Fredonia Inn
200 N. Fredonia Street
Nacogdoches, TX 76961
(409) 564-4665

The best accommodations in Nacogdoches are here. A Quality Inn motel, the Fredonia offers a choice of three styles of rooms: motel, hotel, or cabana. The Inn also has a full restaurant, lounge, and banquet/meeting facilities. Bikes are permitted in the motel and cabana rooms. This and the Inn's central location, just one block from the town square, make the Fredonia the ideal choice.

There are two other motels in Nacogdoches: the Continental with 80 rooms on TX 59 North and the Holiday Inn with 138 rooms, also on TX 59 North.

What to See

THE OLD STONE FORT

Referred to in the earliest records as "Stone House," it was built in 1779 and is almost as old as the city itself. From the walls of this fort have flown eight flags: the Royal Flag of Spain, the flag of the Megee-Gutierrez Expedition in 1813, the flag of Dr. James Long's "Republic" of 1819, the flag of the Republic of Fredonia in 1826, the Mexican flag, the Lone Star flag of the Texas Republic in 1838, the Confederate flag, and the Union Stars and Stripes.

The fort was built by Gil Y'Barbo as a trading post and has since been the center of nearly every historical event that has occurred in East Texas. Beginning as a trading post, the fort served as Spanish troop headquarters in 1806, the seat of government of the Eastern Provinces of Spain in 1810, the home of the first two newspapers in Texas and as a storehouse for court records until 1840. The battle of Nacogdoches was fought on this site in 1832 when the Mexican Army demanded that the citizenry relinquish their guns. The Mexican commander, Col. Jose de las Piedras, finally settled the issue by allowing the citizens to keep their arms provided they were not used against his troops. The Colonel, I'm sure, later regretted this compromise.

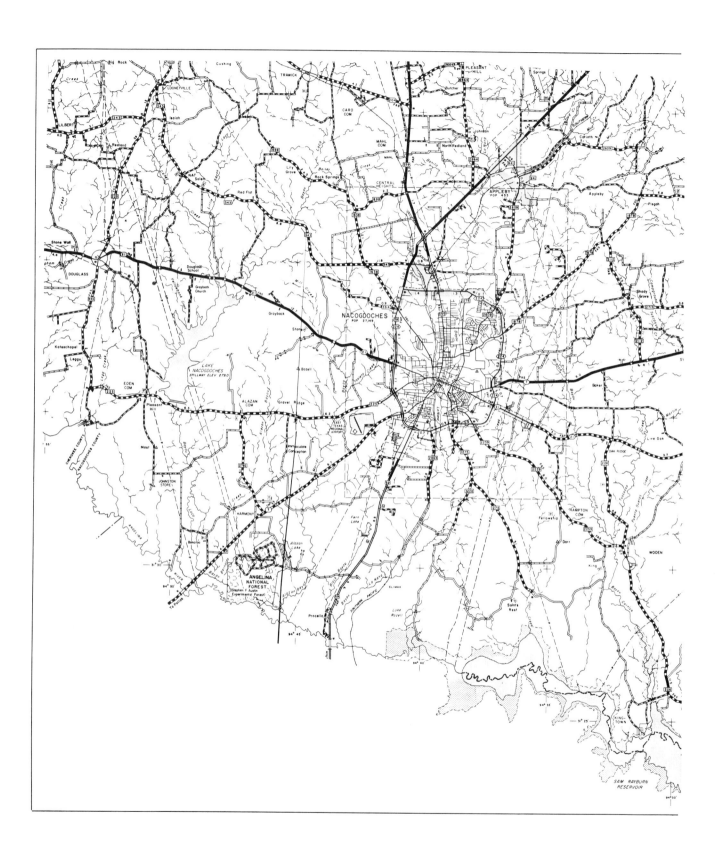

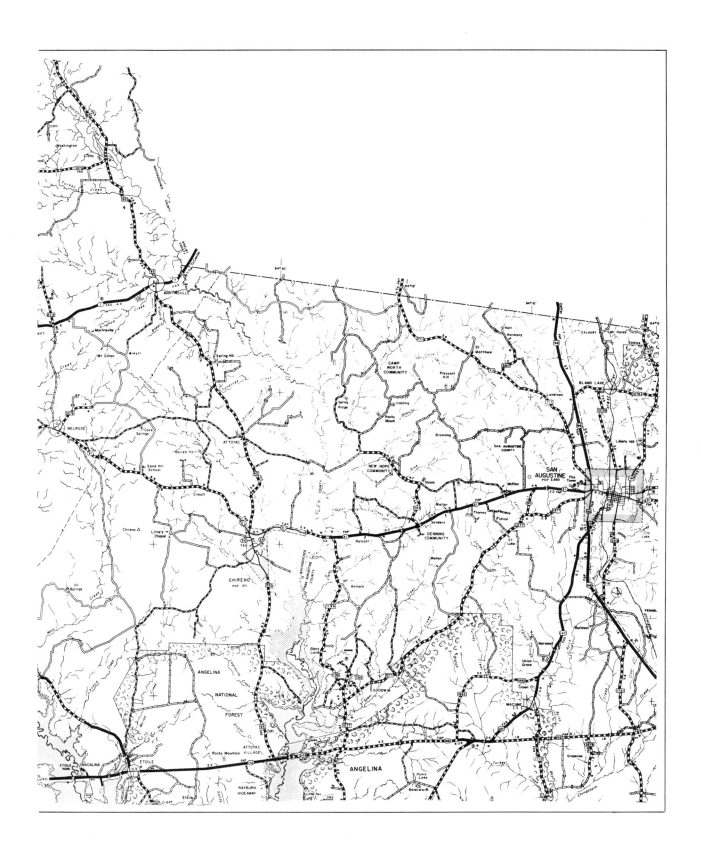

After Texas became a state, the fort was the location for the first district court. In 1907 The Old Stone Fort was moved to the campus of Nacogdoches High School, and in 1936 moved to its present location on the campus of Stephen F. Austin State University.

HOYA MEMORIAL LIBRARY AND MUSEUM

The history of this house embraces the history of East Texas, from the earliest "white" colonization, to the Texas Revolution and the founding of the Texas Republic. Also known as the Adolphus Sterne Home, it was the center for the social, political, and military life of that period. The house was built in 1828 by Adolphus Sterne and was the first permanent residence in the area. Today, the front rooms, the room behind the Sam Houston Room, the back porch, the mantels, and floors are all original.

Sam Houston was baptized in the home in May 1833 with Mrs. Sterne as his godmother. Adolphus Sterne died in 1852, and the house was sold to Joseph vanderHoya in 1869. He lived there until his death in 1897. Today, memorabilia from Sterne, Hoya, and Sam Houston can be seen on display.

OAK GROVE CEMETERY

In this cemetery are the graves of four signers of the Texas Declaration of Independence: Thomas J. Rusk; Charles S. Taylor; John S. Roberts, one of the owners of the Old Stone Fort; and William S. Clark (Clark's monument is known as the "Angel Marker"). The oldest grave is dated 1837.

OLD NACOGDOCHES UNIVERSITY BUILDING

The University was founded by the Republic of Texas on February 3, 1845 and is believed to be the first nonsectarian institution in the state. The present building was erected in 1859. During the Civil War, it served as a hospital and headquarters for both Confederate and Union soldiers. It has been a Catholic school, a lodge, and today is a museum open at unspecified hours. The original building is located on the campus of Nacogdoches High School.

THE HOYA LAND OFFICE

Built in 1897 by Charles Hoya, it is located on the main square at the corner of Pilar and Pecan streets. The land office was used as a fireproof repository for land records that had accumulated since the days of the Texas Republic. The building is one of the first ever built to be truly fireproof, with double brick walls and floors and ceiling of steel reinforced concrete.

OLD NORTH CHURCH

Built in 1838 on the site where the first Protestant services in Texas were held, it was originally known as the Union Church. Today, it is the property of the Missionary Baptists, with services still being regularly held.

INDIAN MOUND OAK

The last of four mounds that were located along Mound Street. The mounds were built for ceremonial purposes or burial spots. During the building of Nacogdoches University, three of the mounds were leveled.

MILLARD'S CROSSING

Here, in a community setting, is a collection of eight of the oldest homes in Nacogdoches. The homes have each been completely restored and furnished with antiques of the period.

There are two guided tours daily, Monday through Saturday, 9:30 a.m. and 2:00 p.m. and Sunday at 2:00 p.m. only. Special group tours may be arranged in advance by calling (409) 564-6631. Millard's Crossing is open all year.

LA CALLE DEL NORTE

Better known as North Street (US 59) in Nacogdoches, it is the oldest street in North America, outside of Mexico. Called La Calle del Norte by the Spanish, it originally led from the Nacogdoches Indian Village to the Nasonite Indian Village near present-day Cushing (about 20 miles north). Today, the only remaining section of this street is in Nacogdoches. (Caution: The heaviest traffic is on this street.)

City Tour

Any tour of the city of Nacogdoches should begin with the Hoya Museum. This is the best source of historical information in the city. The knowledgeable volunteers are always eager to share their information with everyone.

From the Fredonia Inn at the corner of North Fredonia and Hospital Streets, go east on Hospital Street for 3 blocks to Walker Street. Turn south on Walker Street for one block to Main Street (TX 21). Turn east on Main Street for one block to the red light and turn south on Lanana Street. The Hoya Museum is located two blocks down at the end of this street.

Leaving the museum, return to Main Street and continue straight on Lanana Street for two blocks to the Oak Grove Cemetery. This is the final resting place of Thomas J. Rusk, first Secretary of War for the Republic of Texas. The Rusk Memorial is located in the southwest corner of the cemetery, easily seen from Lanana Street. Also buried here are three other signers of the Texas Declaration of Independence and others who helped shape the destiny of Texas. In the northwest corner is located the Zion Hill First Baptist Church, a classic example of the designs of German architect Dietrich Rulfs.

Backtrack on Lanana Street for one-half block to Price Street (opposite the main gate of the cemetery) and turn west for one block to Mound Street. Turn north on Mound Street, and note all the splendid examples of Victorian homes on your right. On the left is the campus of Nacogdoches High School with the Old Nacogdoches University Building visible. Opposite this campus, on a private residence, is the last Indian mound. The mound is marked by a historical marker. Continue on Mound Street, which dead ends at Starr Avenue. Turn east and then north again into the divided street named Clark Boulevard. This road is on the campus of Stephen F. Austin State University and will lead you directly to the Old Stone Fort. The fort is open Monday through Satur-

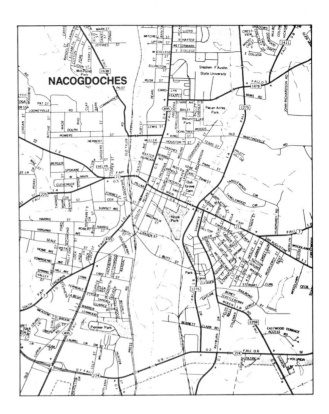

day from 9:00 a.m. to 5:00 p.m. and Sunday from 1:00 p.m. to 5:00 p.m.

From here, ride through the campus and one block east to Raquet Street and turn north for about one-and-a-half miles to Burrows Street. Turn west on Burrows to North Street (US 59) and head north on North Street for 2 miles to Old Post Oak Road and Millard's Crossing. This fascinating collection of historic homes is open year round, and the tours are free.

Returning to US 59, go north over the railroad tracks to the next little road and exit to the right (east). A short distance down this bumpy road is the Old North Church. A tour through the adjoining cemetery may be of interest as well. Note the historical markers under the large tree in front of the church. This church has been at this same location, celebrating religious services for over 140 years.

The Old North Church is located about four miles north of downtown. To return take the same route out and a second look at the historic locations, or ride south on US 59 past Burrows Street to Lakewood Street and turn west one block to Pearl Street. Follow Pearl all the way to Main. This route is a restful ride through residential areas. Turn east on Main into the brick streets of downtown. In the main square is the public library. On the southwest corner is a historical marker set into the cornerstone of the bank marking the original location of the Old Stone Fort. Riding north on Church Street, you will go past a beautiful example of a high Victorian mansion, the Roland Jones House, built in 1896 by architect Dietrich Rulfs.

Across the street is the Fredonia Inn and the end of the city tour. The total distance is approximately 10 miles.

An evening ride down Mound Street to the Stephen F. Austin University campus and back is a very pleasant way to end a day of touring this most historic of Texas cities.

TOUR #1
Looneyville - Douglass

ROUTE
US 259 north - .3 miles
FM 1638 west - 4.6 miles
FM 343 west - 13.6 miles
FM 225 south - 25.5 miles

DISTANCE
44.0 miles/70.4 kilometers

TERRAIN
Gently rolling to rolling

TRAFFIC
Nil, except on north US 259

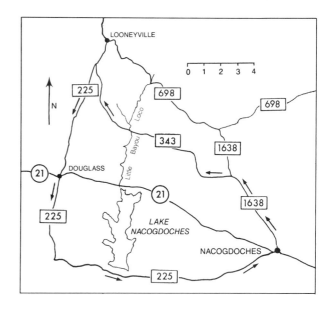

The intersection of US 259 (the north end of North Street) and FM 1638 (Powers Street) is, for some reason, the easiest junction to miss in this entire book! I have missed it four times, and I know exactly where it is. Your tendency is to "go with the flow" on North Street and not to watch for the sign. The junction is also closer to the main intersection than you realize. Read the following directions closely.

Northbound on US 259 from the stop light at the junction with TX 7 and TX 21, the first cross street is Hospital Street. The next cross street is Mimms Street, then the next *left* is Muller Street. The next *left* is Powers Street, alias FM 1638. Turn here. The total distance is less than a half of a mile.

On FM 1638, it's 2.5 miles to the loop. Continue straight for another 2.1 miles to the junction with FM 343. Turn left onto FM 343.

The next 12.5 miles to Looneyville gently roll through stands of pines and farm land. You will cross two bridges along this section—the first over Bayou Loco and the second over Little Bayou Loco. The scenery at the bayous changes dramatically. The stands of pine are replaced by moss-laden cypress and oak that crowd closely to the water's edge often overhanging the bayou. Seen from the air, the bayous would appear as lush dense intrusions in the homogeneous pine forests.

In Looneyville, there is only a gas station/grocery store. Here also, you come to another perplexing farm road junction. To the right is FM 225. To the left is FM 343 and FM 225. Turn *left,* and 1.2 miles further FM 343 breaks off the right. Continue straight on FM 225 towards Douglass.

FM 225 will take you all the way back into Nacogdoches by a somewhat circuitous route. In Douglass, stock up on water and snacks because there will be nothing for the next 18 miles or so. Five miles south of Douglass, FM 225 takes a sharp left turn. At the junction on the right side is a historical marker. About 3 miles further is Lake Nacogdoches and the best winding downhill on the route.

From the dam, back into town, the road is winding and gently rolling. On a weekend, in good weather, there may be increased traffic. Even so, traffic is still light.

This tour can be split into two tours at Douglass. Instead of following FM 225, you can turn left (east) onto TX 21. However, there are three *big* hills to climb. If you like climbing hills, then take a left. If you prefer a less strenuous route, stay on FM 225. Choosing TX 21 saves only about 5 miles on the original route. The hills are more challenging.

TOUR #2
Shady Grove

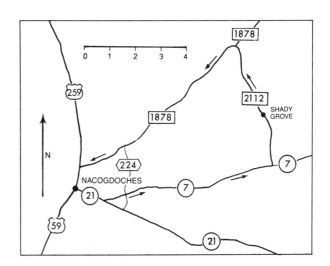

ROUTE

TX 7 east - 8.0 miles
FM 2112 north - 5.0 miles
FM 1878 west - 8.3 miles

DISTANCE

21.3 miles/34.1 kilometers

TERRAIN

Gently rolling to rolling

TRAFFIC

Light to nil

TX 7 is a busy road within the loop around Nacogdoches, but I have found the drivers there to be very courteous.

The biggest hill to climb on the entire route is right in town. Although the hill is steep, it is mercifully short. Once past Orten Hill, follow TX 7 to the left at the "Y" junction with TX 21. About 1 mile further is Loop 224. Once past this junction, TX 7 becomes a typical East Texas highway, i.e., surrounded with pines, open farm land, and rolling hills. Five miles past the loop is the turnoff on FM 2112 north.

A left turn takes you onto FM 2112 where you can relax, enjoy the ride and sail along this

winding road. You may want to stop and explore at the Shady Grove Church and Cemetery. Most of the cemeteries in East Texas are old enough to be historically interesting, and this is one of those that is. FM 2112 is about as peaceful as a paved road can be, so enjoy it while you are there.

At the junction with FM 1878, turn left and follow the curve. This peculiar intersection somehow transforms from FM 2112 to FM 1878. Well whatever it is, take a left and continue southwest on FM 1878.

This fun road dips and plunges for 5.5 miles back to the loop. Continue straight past the loop, through residential areas, to US 259. Turn left onto US 259 and return to the main square.

TOUR #3
Martinsville - Chireno

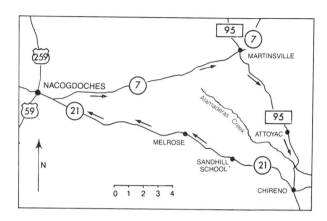

ROUTE
TX 7 east - 14 miles
FM 95 south - 11 miles
TX 21 east - .1 miles
Loop 34 - 1.5 miles
TX 21 west - 22.8 miles

DISTANCE
49.4 miles/79 kilometers

TERRAIN
Gently rolling to rolling

TRAFFIC
Usually light, except on Saturdays

Tour #3 begins on Main Street square downtown and heads east on TX 7 and TX 21. The road crosses Lanana Bayou and climbs sharply up Orten Hill, which is the steepest section of the tour. Once on top, the road levels out and a half mile further is the "Y" junction of TX 7 and TX 21. Go left on TX 7 to another less obvious "Y" about a mile further on. TX 7 leads to the left and a small, barely paved road leads right. Three-and-one-quarter miles down this road is a historic house built in 1833 and still occupied today (this side tour is not included in the tour distance).

Continuing on TX 7, the road rolls alternately through pine forests and open farm land. Numerous vistas open up along the route as the road gains elevation to the high point of the tour at Swift. Just east of Swift is one of the finest overlooks in the area, followed immediately by a long plunge downhill. Coming into the little town of Martinsville (El. 284 ft.), continue just past the turn south on Hwy 95 to the general store on the left. Refreshments are available here. Turning south on Hwy 95 begins a very peaceful, unhurried ride for 12 miles to Chireno. This section of the route is one of the most pleasant to ride. Near

the end of this section, about 2.5 miles south of Attoyac, is a bridge crossing Amaladeras Creek, the lowest point of the tour (El. 235 ft.). Shortly after this bridge is the junction with TX 21. Turn east here for .8 mile to Loop 34 into Chireno. Turn south and the Loop will lead directly into town. Along this short section, on the left, is one of the best examples of Victorian Gingerbread architecture in the country, according to *Architectural Digest*. On the southwest corner of the junction of Loop 34 and TX 95 is an old house which has been converted into a restaurant that makes an excellent lunch spot.

Chireno was first settled in 1837 and is best known for being the location of the first oil discovery in Texas. In 1867, two hunters noticed oil trickling from the banks of a small creek branch. The oil was originally used on saddles and harnesses.

The tour continues on TX 95 north to the junction with TX 21. Turn west on TX 21 and about one mile further on the right is the site of the Old Midway Inn. Built in 1836, this stagecoach inn was the halfway stop between Nacogdoches and San Augustine, and such Texas heroes as Sam Houston and William Travis stayed here. The lumber used to erect this stately inn came to Jefferson by riverboat and overland by oxcart, and the work was done by slaves. Unfortunately, the main building was moved to a private ranch in 1984, and only a few outbuildings remain at the original site. The historic structure that sat in this original location for 148 years is no longer available for public viewing.

The tour returns past Sand Hill and Melrose, a refreshment stop. Rolling through the red hills of East Texas, the tour connects again with TX 7. This time, you get to ride down Orten Hill, but watch for the red light just past the bottom.

TOUR #4
San Augustine

ROUTE
TX 21 east - 36 miles
TX 21 west - .8 miles
US 96 south - .1 mile
FM 1277 west - 15.4 miles
TX 103 west - 8.5 miles
FM 226 north - 12.2 miles
FM 2259 west - 10.2 miles
TX 21 west - .7 miles

DISTANCE
83.9 miles/134.3 kilometers

TERRAIN
Gently rolling to flat

TRAFFIC
Light to nil

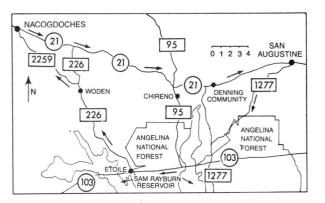

This restored log cabin dates from the early nineteenth century. It is located on TX 21 on Tour #4.

This tour, like Tours #2 and #3, necessitates a climb up Orten Hill. It is still the toughest hill on the tour. At the "Y" junction with TX 7, follow TX 21 to the right and settle in for the long ride to San Augustine.

After passing Loop 224, it is 9 miles of pine-lined, scenic highway to Melrose. Here is the first "watering hole."

Continuing on TX 21, past the Sand Hill School, the next stop is a side trip into Chireno. At the junction of TX 21 and FM 95, turn right to Chireno. Past the "main" block of town is the junction with Loop 34. On the right is a house converted into a restaurant with excellent meals. Turn left onto Loop 34. At the bottom of the hill, on the right, and set back off the road, is a fine example of Victorian Ginger-bread architecture. Continue on the loop back to TX 21 and turn right. The side trip to Chireno adds only .9 mile to the route and is well worth it. This is your last chance to stock up on food and water for the next 15-mile stretch to San Augustine.

Architectural Digest called this one of the five best examples of Victorian gingerbread architecture in the United States. Located on the loop in Chireno, it is a "must-see" for Tours #3 and #4.

In San Augustine, TX 21 crosses US 96. This is the only north-south US highway with an even number. US 96 begins in Port Arthur and ends about 30 miles north of San Augustine in the town of Tenaha. Here it becomes US 59 North.

Continue on TX 21 into the main square of town where the Bank of San Augustine sits on northeast corner of the square. On the front of the bank is a sundial, the only bank sundial in Texas.

After a good rest and a leisurely cruise through town, return to US 96 via TX 21. Turn left (south) onto US 96 and less than .1 mile on the right is FM 1277.

Almost at once, everything changes. There is no traffic, the road seems narrower, and the trees are thicker and closer to the road. The latter half of FM 1277 skirts the northern edge of the Angelina National Forest. It is difficult to distinguish between being in and out of the National Forest because it all looks the same. This is a tribute to those "unprotected" landowners who take care of their natural resources. FM 1277 eventually turns sharply left at the junction with FM 3316 and FM 1196. Shortly after FM 1277 reenters Angelina National Forest, it reaches TX 103, where you should turn right (west) onto TX 103.

Here the roadway again changes dramatically. The highway is very wide and the forest is cut well back from the roadway. If there is wind, you will know it along TX 103. This would have to be considered the "less-enjoyable-cycling" portion of this route. But, take heart, there is a nice (albeit windy) crossing of Lake Sam Rayburn and only 5.5 miles to go to Etoile.

Just past the businesses of Etoile is the junction with FM 226. Once again, there is an instant change of atmosphere as you ride back onto a more typical, narrow farm road with no traffic and close in trees. Be sure to rest well in Etoile, however, because the road will be more rolling again. I find that there is something about cycling through pine trees on a narrow, winding road that makes the hills seem a little less difficult. From Etoile it is 11.5 miles to the next refreshment stop at Woden and the junction with FM 2259.

The last 9 or so miles on FM 2259 into Nacogdoches are as serene as the first 11 miles. FM 2259 passes Loop 224 and reconnects with TX 21. Don't forget the stop light just past the bottom of Orten Hill.

Jefferson

Where to Stay

CAMPING

Primitive camping sites are available at the Nance's Boat Tour grounds, located just across the bayou from Jefferson's historic riverfront district on FM 134. Cross on the Polk Street Bridge and turn right. Boat rides on Big Cypress Bayou are also available for $3 per person for the 45-minute ride.

Contact: Chuck or John Nance
　　　　　Rt. 1, Box 1
　　　　　Jefferson, TX 75657
　　　　　(214) 665-2222

Caddo Lake State Park, located 13 miles east of Jefferson on FM 134, also offers full camping facilities as well as cabins. Canoeing, hiking, and fishing are also available.

Contact: Park Headquarters
　　　　　Caddo Lake State Park
　　　　　Rt. 2, Box 15
　　　　　Karnack, TX 75661
　　　　　(214) 679-3351

MOTELS

Excelsior House (ca. 1850s)
211 W. Austin Street
(214) 665-2513

Facilities: 14 rooms and 2 suites. Make reservations a minimum of 6 months in advance for weekends. No bicycles are permitted inside the rooms or on the grounds.

New Jefferson Inn (ca. 1861)
124 W. Austin
(214) 665-2631

Facilities: 22 rooms. Call well in advance for reservations. Ask if bikes are allowed.

Sherry Inn Motel
Hwy 59 South
(214) 665-2581

Facilities: 33 rooms, color TV, private club. Bicycles allowed.

BED AND BREAKFAST INNS

Hale House (in the Historic District)
702 S. Line St.
(214) 665-8877

Facilities: 5 rooms. Mark and Linda Leonard, proprietors.

Pride House (ca. 1888)
409 Broadway
(214) 665-2675

Facilities: Rooms with private bath. Ruthmary Jordan, proprietor.

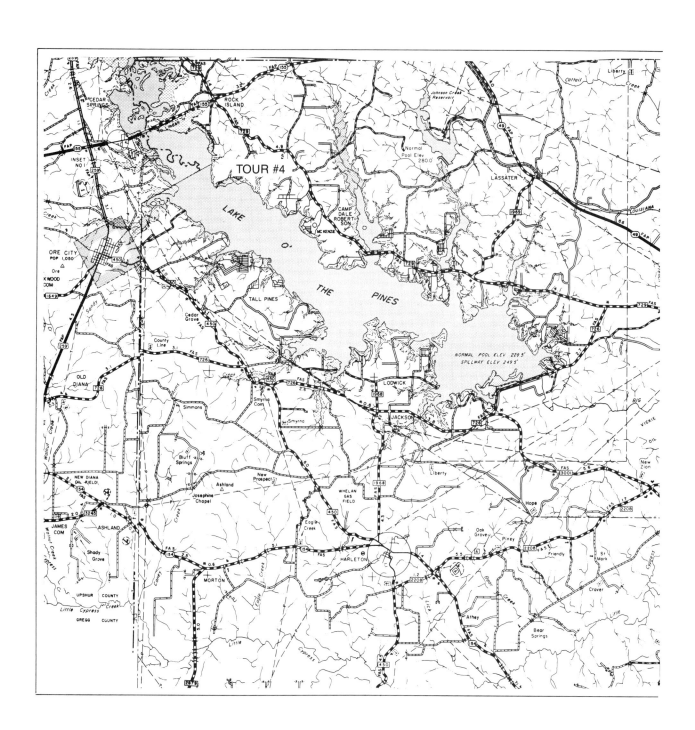

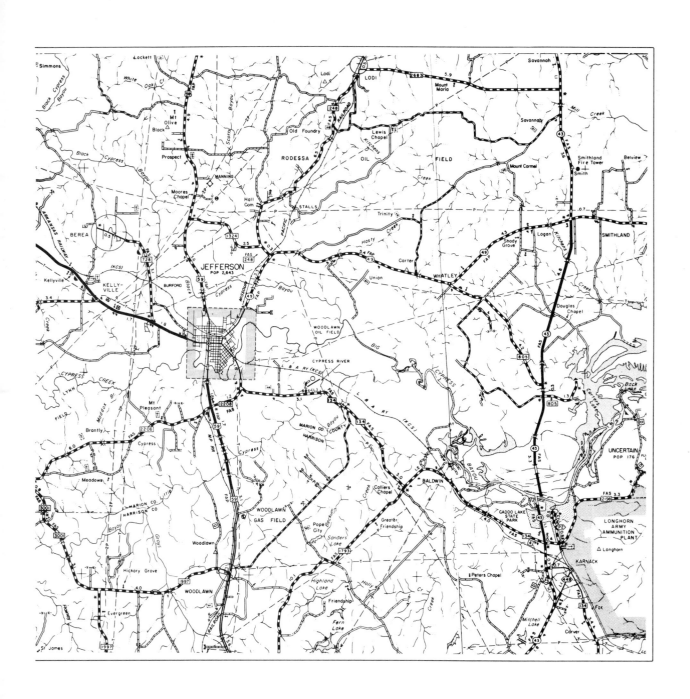

Wise Manor
312 Houston St.
(214) 665-7161

Facilities: 2 rooms with double bed, 1 room with single bed.

The Cottage
307 Soda St.
(214) 665-8572 or 665-2753

Facilities: Newly restored Victorian cottage with a selection of rooms and a sitting area.

Collins House
409 S. Alley St.
(214) 665-2483

Facilities: One suite with sitting room and kitchenette. Private porch. Additional separate bedroom.

The Magnolias (ca. 1867)
209 E. Broadway
(214) 665-2754

Built by Dan N. Alley, cofounder of Jefferson, for his daughter, Victoria.

What to See

A complete list of the more than 80 historic and other sites in Jefferson can be obtained from the map provided by the chamber of commerce (See the "Appendix" for the chamber's address.)

City Tour

Any tour of Jefferson must include the Historic District along the riverfront. The chamber of commerce is located here, next to the new Jefferson Inn. Other than this specific area, there are a total of 84 historic sites in and around Jefferson. Most of the locations are included on the map. For a complete listing, contact the chamber of commerce as listed in the Appendix.

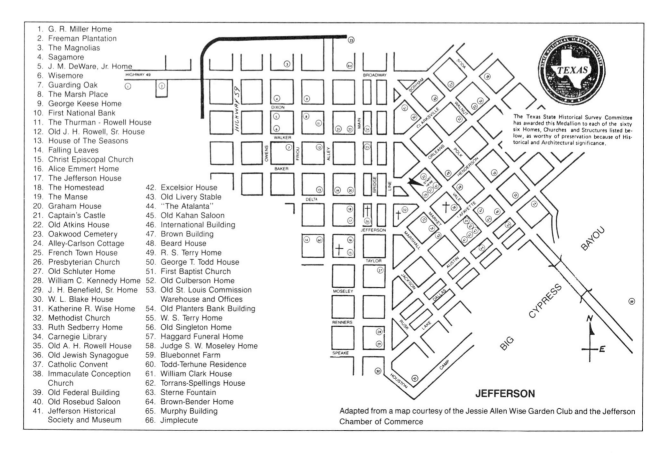

1. G. R. Miller Home
2. Freeman Plantation
3. The Magnolias
4. Sagamore
5. J. M. DeWare, Jr. Home
6. Wisemore
7. Guarding Oak
8. The Marsh Place
9. George Keese Home
10. First National Bank
11. The Thurman - Rowell House
12. Old J. H. Rowell, Sr. House
13. House of The Seasons
14. Falling Leaves
15. Christ Episcopal Church
16. Alice Emmert Home
17. The Jefferson House
18. The Homestead
19. The Manse
20. Graham House
21. Captain's Castle
22. Old Atkins House
23. Oakwood Cemetery
24. Alley-Carlson Cottage
25. French Town House
26. Presbyterian Church
27. Old Schluter Home
28. William C. Kennedy Home
29. J. H. Benefield, Sr. Home
30. W. L. Blake House
31. Katherine R. Wise Home
32. Methodist Church
33. Ruth Sedberry Home
34. Carnegie Library
35. Old A. H. Rowell House
36. Old Jewish Synagogue
37. Catholic Convent
38. Immaculate Conception Church
39. Old Federal Building
40. Old Rosebud Saloon
41. Jefferson Historical Society and Museum
42. Excelsior House
43. Old Livery Stable
44. "The Atalanta"
45. Old Kahan Saloon
46. International Building
47. Brown Building
48. Beard House
49. R. S. Terry Home
50. George T. Todd House
51. First Baptist Church
52. Old Culberson Home
53. Old St. Louis Commission Warehouse and Offices
54. Old Planters Bank Building
55. W. S. Terry Home
56. Old Singleton Home
57. Haggard Funeral Home
58. Judge S. W. Moseley Home
59. Bluebonnet Farm
60. Todd-Terhune Residence
61. William Clark House
62. Torrans-Spellings House
63. Sterne Fountain
64. Brown-Bender Home
65. Murphy Building
66. Jimplecute

Adapted from a map courtesy of the Jessie Allen Wise Garden Club and the Jefferson Chamber of Commerce

TOUR #1
Lodi - Mill Creek

ROUTE
TX 49 north - 3.3 miles
FM 248 west - 6.8 miles
FM 2683 east - 5.9 miles
TX 43 south - .7 miles
Unnamed dirt road west - 8.5 miles
TX 49 west - 4.1 miles

DISTANCE
29.3 miles/46.9 kilometers

TERRAIN
Gently rolling

TRAFFIC
Light to nil

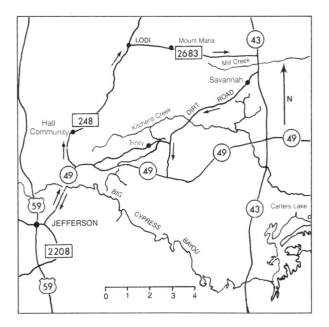

This plantation home is found east of Jefferson on FM 134.

This tour is the easiest to circle in the area. It also is the prettiest. Starting in the center of town, ride north on TX 49 to the junction of FM 248. There turn left towards Lodi and continue on FM 248 past the community of Hall. The road winds peacefully through the East Texas woods.

In Lodi, be sure to stock up on water and food as there is nowhere to get these again until Jefferson. Also in Lodi is the junction with FM 2683. Turn right.

FM 2683 is a marvelous road that displays the simplicity of the area. The Mount Maria Church is roughly halfway to the next junction. This section of the route is much straighter than the previous sections, but it still retains the intimacy offered by the enclosing forest.

At the junction with TX 43, turn right. The next turn is a little harder to find, so read the following directions carefully. After the turn onto TX 43, you will cross a bridge over Mill Creek. Two-tenths of a mile further is a small unnamed lane that leads to the right. It is the first road to the right, past the bridge. This road becomes unpaved, but is in excellent shape—smooth and well-drained.

About one mile down this road is the Savannah Church on the right, and a short distance further is a "Y" junction. Follow the road to the left. This section offers a relaxing and serene ride under a canopy of trees. This road carries you as deep into the forest as you can go on a bike. Even this "dirt" road is a better road than many "paved" roads.

After the second bridge (across Kitchens Creek), the road makes a big curve to the left. Very shortly after this curve is a road to the right that will lead past the Trinity Church. (There may be a sign to the church.) Take this road to the right, but if you miss it, don't worry. You will still end up at TX 49. Continuing past Trinity Church, there are still two-and-a-half to three miles of the most pleasant cycling in the area. Enjoy it; TX 49 brings you back to reality.

The junction at TX 49 is rather nondescript. Simply turn right and follow TX 49 back into Jefferson.

TOUR #2
Caddo Lake State Park

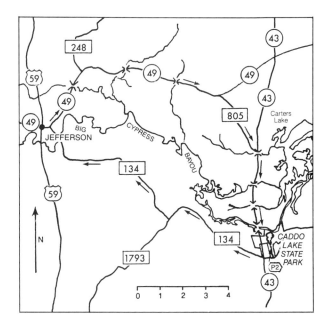

ROUTE
  TX 49 north - 8.7 miles
  FM 805 east - 4.2 miles
  TX 43 south - 4.7 miles
  FM 134 east - .4 miles
  Park Road P2 - 3.2 miles
  FM 134 west - 13.5 miles

DISTANCE
  34.7 miles/55.5 kilometers

TERRAIN
  Gently rolling

TRAFFIC
  Light

This tour will cross the bayous used by the great riverboats that brought products from and to New Orleans in the early days of Texas. Follow TX 49 north past the Lodi junction. The road dips and rolls through the pines and has a couple of brisk climbs. TX 49 will curve sharply to the left at the junction with FM 805. Turn right on FM 805.

The forests immediately close in on the road, which is typical of the farm roads of this area. This road connects TX 49 and TX 43 before the state highways join further north. Farm roads have less traffic and provide more enjoyable cycling, anyway.

At the junction with TX 43, turn right. This highway crosses three bayous, the last of which is Big Cypress Bayou, the original route of the riverboats from Caddo Lake into Jefferson. About a mile-and-a-half further is the junction with FM 134. If you want to skip Caddo Lake State Park altogether, then turn right. The savings are about 4 miles; the loss is all yours. A trip through the state park is a must.

Turn left onto FM 134 for .4 (four-tenths) mile to the entrance of the park on the left. The round trip through the park is 3.2 miles and the usual fee for bicycles in a state park is 50 cents. How can you go wrong for 50 cents?

The last half of the park road drops steeply to the lake. *Caution!* At the bottom of the steep hill, the road turns sharply to the left. (To the right is the road to the boat ramp.) This road is narrow and fast. It may be advisable to take the easier right and then turn around.

At the start of the camping area is a small cabin that sells soft drinks and fishing gear and rents canoes. The road loops around through the campsites and begins the ascent of that wonderful downhill plunge you just enjoyed. The ride back to the park headquarters is strenuous enough to get you out of breath. It is what I call a "huff-n-puff."

Return to the entrance and turn right onto FM 134. Cross TX 43 and follow FM 134 all the way back into Jefferson. Along the way, you will cross several small bayous and Little Cypress Bayou, a tributary of Big Cypress Bayou.

The route enters town across Big Cypress Bayou again at the terminus of the riverboat route. This manmade enlargement is called the Turning Basin. It is also the most historic end of town.

TOUR #3
Lake O' The Pines Dam

ROUTE
TX 49 west - 3.5 miles
FM 729 west - 3.4 miles
FM 726 south - 5.0 miles
FM 3001 east - 5.6 miles
FM 2208 east - 7.2 miles
FM 134 north - 1.8 miles

DISTANCE
26.5 miles/42.4 kilometers

TERRAIN
Gently rolling to rolling

TRAFFIC
Light to nil

Jefferson is located between two beautiful, but very different lakes. Caddo Lake to the east is more like a swamp or jungle. Lake O' The Pines, to the west, is typical of East Texas lakes with large pines and open waters.

The tour begins on TX 49 westbound to the small community of Kellyville. Turn left onto FM 729. After the light traffic of TX 49, the change is dramatic—FM 729 is almost deserted. As you roll through the pine trees to the junction with FM 726, relax and enjoy the scenery. At the junction turn left on FM 726.

The Spanish moss and junglelike forests create a mysterious and timeless world within Caddo Lake State Park.

This road will cross the lake dam. Watch for the eagles that live in this area. There is no greater feeling of freedom than to cycle through the low, rolling hills and pine forest and see an eagle soaring above.

The dam itself is about a mile long and offers a great view of the lake and the surrounding forest along the entire length. Just past the end of the dam is the junction with FM 3001. There is a store at this junction. Turn left onto FM 3001.

The entire trip back into Jefferson is along casual farm roads with low, rolling hills and close-in forests. Turn left onto FM 2208 and continue the winding route past streams and fields to the junction with US 59. This is the busiest highway in Texas except for the interstates. Continue straight on FM 2208 to FM 134. Turn left back into Jefferson.

TOUR #4
Around Lake O' The Pines

ROUTE
TX 49 west - 3.5 miles
FM 729 west - 17.4 miles
TX 155 west - 3.9 miles
US 259 south - 3.1 miles
FM 450 east - 6.0 miles
FM 726 east - 8.1 miles
FM 3001 east - 5.6 miles
FM 2208 east - 7.2 miles
FM 134 north - 1.8 miles

DISTANCE
56.6 miles/90.6 kilometers

TERRAIN
Gently rolling to rolling

TRAFFIC
Moderate to nil

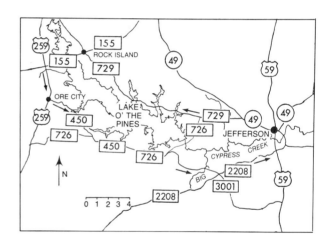

This tour is one of those that is great only after you have finished it. You are glad you did it, but you would not do it a second time. Personally, I like to circumnavigate lakes. If you feel the same, then enjoy. But if you do not like traffic, take Tour #3.

The primary traffic problems occur on the following sections: TX 155, US 259, and FM 450. These three will have moderate traffic. FM 729 from the junction with FM 726 to TX 155 has light traffic as does FM 726 from FM 450 to FM 3001.

There are some terrific views as you cross the numerous arms of the lake, and its does give you a true sense of accomplishment to have finished the route. But, this tour is included as a "mixed" tour. The scenery is often grand, but the traffic is busy. If you want to test your handling skills, this is the route to choose.

Kerrville/Fredericksburg

Where to Stay and Eat

The Kerrville Convention and Visitors Bureau offers a guide to dining and accommodations in the area. The following are recommended:

CAMPING

Kerrville State Park is a complete camping resort open all year round. It stretches more than 500 acres from Flat Rock Lake to the hills where deer come down to feed in the evening.

MOTELS

Del Norte Inn
708 Junction Hwy 27 West
(512) 257-6112

All rooms are at ground level, and cyclists are very welcome. Excellent dining adjacent to the motel.

DINING

Fara's International
1201 Broadway
(512) 896-6580

This is one of the best restaurants in the area. It serves excellent lasagne and other pastas as well as steaks and seafood. It is not inexpensive, but it is a treat well deserved after a day's cycling.

What to See

THE CHARLES SCHREINER MANSION

Built in 1879 and now completely restored, the mansion is the home of the Hill Country Museum. The museum is located next to the Post Office on Earl Garrett Street and is open every day except Wednesday from 2:00 p.m. to 4:30 p.m.

BICYCLES, ETC.

Located across the street from the museum, at 233 Earl Garrett Street, (zip: 78028, phone: (512) 896-6864). Owned by Dick and Sarah Mauldin, it is a great place to meet and learn more about hill country cycling, not to mention picking up those extra ditties you forgot to pack! Their hours are 8:00–5:30 Monday–Friday and 9:00–4:00 Saturday.

PAMPELL'S PHARMACY:

Located at 701 Water Street at Sidney Baker (TX 16). This building was originally an opera house and has a historic marker on the corner that tells the story. The interior has changed little since it became a pharmacy after the turn of the century. It still boasts an old fashioned soda fountain.

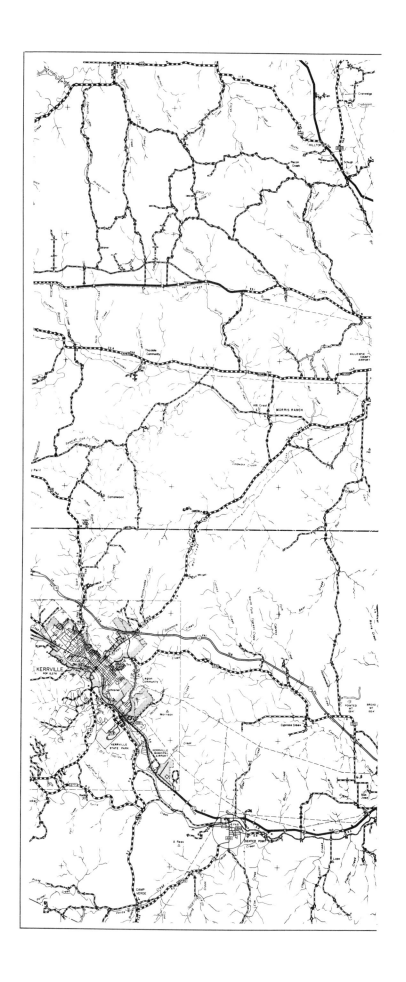

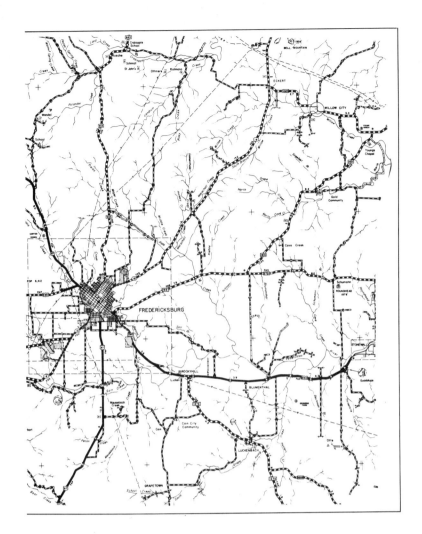

COWBOY ARTISTS OF AMERICA MUSEUM

Located at 1550 Bandera Highway between Kerrville and the Kerrville State Park. The museum houses a changing collection of art by the nation's top Western artists, including Frederic Remington and Charles Russell. If you like art and the west, then this museum is a "must see." Admission is $2 for adults.

Three annual events of particular note are as follows:

TEXAS STATE ARTS AND CRAFTS FAIR

This is held in May and June. For more information contact

TACF
P.O. Box 1527,
Kerrville, TX 78028
(512) 896-5711

KERRVILLE WINTER MUSIC FESTIVAL

This is held from December to March. Contact the chamber of commerce for further information.

EASTER HILL COUNTRY TOUR

Held each year on Easter weekend, this bicycle tour attracts cyclists from all across the state and country. Three days of rides with different routes to choose from are offered. A century ride (100 miles) on Saturday is also included. Be sure to register well in advance and reserve your campsite at the state park early. Contact Dick Mauldin at Bicycles, Etc., listed above, for more information and registration forms.

City Tours

KERRVILLE

Kerrville is known for its music festivals and arts and crafts fairs, and if you enjoy those things, you ought to time your visit to coincide with one of them.

A tour of the city is better made on foot than by bike. Begin by parking at the county courthouse, located at 300 Sydney Baker Street (TX 16). On the east side of the courthouse, paralleling Sydney Baker is Earl Garrett Street. Walk south on this street to the Charles Schreiner Mansion, which will be on the right. The tour through the museum here will bring to life the history of the Hill Country.

At the end of the block is the Pampell Pharmacy. Go inside and step back into turn-of-the-century America. Enjoy an old-fashioned soda from the fountain.

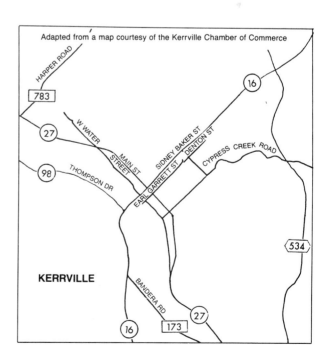

Adapted from a map courtesy of the Kerrville Chamber of Commerce

FREDERICKSBURG

A tour of Fredericksburg can be made when you take Tour #3. The best guide for a fascinating tour of the city is a little book available from the chamber of commerce entitled *Fredericksburg Self-Guiding Auto Tour.* Although called an "auto tour," it is concise enough for cyclists as well. Fully illustrated and with a map in the centerfold, the book provides a full description of the historical district.

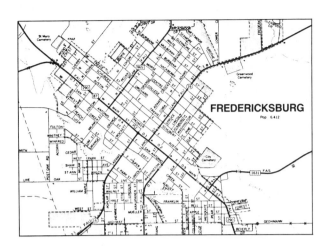

TOUR #1
Kerrville State Park - Turtle Creek

ROUTE
TX 16 south - .8 mile
TX 173 south - 5.9 miles
FM 2771 west - 6.3 miles
TX 16 north - 6.8 miles

DISTANCE
19.8 miles/31.8 kilometers

TERRAIN
Mostly rolling with some hills

TRAFFIC
FM road-none; TX Hwys-light

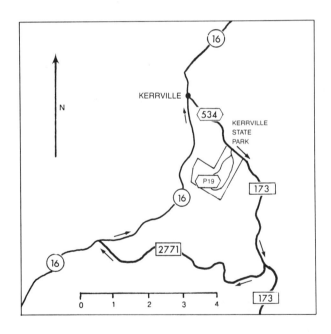

TX 16 is known as Sidney Baker Street through Kerrville. In the vicinity of Kerrville, TX 16 has wide, smooth shoulders which make for relatively safe cycling.

After the junction of TX 16 and TX 173, the latter becomes two narrow lanes with light traf-

fic. Fortunately, most drivers in this area are used to seeing cyclists on the road. Immediately past the junction of TX 173 and Loop 534 is Kerrville State Park. The park has two units, one on either side of the highway. The park headquarters are on the east side. The park is the most popular camping spot in the area, so it is best to make reservations for holiday weekends.

Continuing on TX 173 south, the road runs along the Guadalupe River, crosses Dry Hollow Creek, and 3.8 miles from the park, brings you to the junction with FM 2771.

Turning west on FM 2771 (the only way you *can* turn) the road crosses the pretty opalescent green Turtle Creek twice. FM 2771 offers a very peaceful, gentle ride through low hills and past numerous small ranches, and ends at the junction with TX 16. Turn right, climb three passes in 6.8 miles and you will reach the courthouse.

TOUR #2
Cedar Creek - Camp Verde

ROUTE
TX 16 north - .6 mile
FM 1341 east - 14.9 miles
Cedar Creek Road south - 3.0 miles
Wilson Creek Road west - 3.8 miles
TX 27 west - 1.2 miles
FM 1350 west - 2.2 miles
FM 480 south - 6.5 miles
TX 173 north - 11.1 miles
TX 16 north - .8 mile

DISTANCE
44.2 miles/70.5 kilometers

TERRAIN
Hilly to flat

TRAFFIC
Mostly nil to light

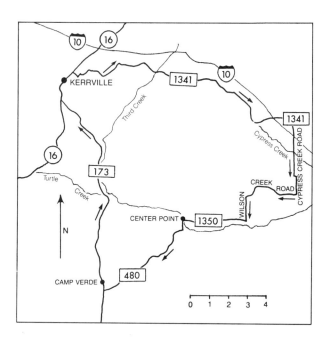

Tx 16 is the major north-south road in Kerrville, with the traffic to prove it. To avoid the traffic and possibly an abrupt end to your tour, take Earl Garrett Street (one block east of TX 16) north and ride parallel to the main thoroughfare. Follow Earl Garrett Street to the "yield" sign and dogleg right then left to Hillcrest Street. Go one block to the stop sign and turn right. You are now on Wheless Street which is also FM 1341. At the bottom of the hill is a stop sign, so be careful. Turn left and you're off for the climb up Mount Tivy. The

climb is only about .3 mile, but is quite steep. At the top is a historical marker telling the story of James Tivy and his family. It provides a good excuse to stop and catch your breath.

Just around the bend is the junction with Loop 534. Ignore it and continue straight on FM 1341. You now enter the tight little valley of Third Creek. That microwave tower ahead is your goal. There is about a one-mile climb to the top of the pass, but the downhill is even longer and a great thrill. From here on, the going is predominantly downhill to flat. The highway to your left is I-10, the most boring road in Texas. FM 1341 continues flat for a couple of pleasant miles, then a short rise reveals the I-10 overpass. There is no access here, but there are some interesting mud nests to look at

This jackrabbit streaking through the under-brush of the Texas Hill Country is one example of the wildlife that can be seen from the quiet, lei-surely comfort of a bicycle.

Lower Crabapple Road (Tour #3) has virtually no traffic, a good surface, gently rolling hills, and frequent wildlife, making it one of the most enjoyable sections to ride in the Kerrville-Fredericksburg area.

as you ride under the bridge. The road will curve back to the right, and 1.8 miles from the underpass, you will cross over I-10, where im-mediately to the left is a dry stone wall built in the early 1900s. Continue straight on the nar-row county road called Cypress Creek Road. A short climb which then drops down and over a low-water crossing of Cypress Creek is fol-lowed by a bridge on which you will cross the creek again. About 1.9 miles from the over-pass, the road will angle sharply left. Take the next paved road, .1 mile further, to the right. In .9 mile you will come to an intersection and turn right. Straight ahead is a low-water cross-ing with a black-and-white warning barrier. A sign post on the right side indicates that TX 27 is straight ahead, Cypress Creek Road is the road you are now on, and Wilson Creek Road is to the right. Turn right onto Wilson Creek Road.

Along this 3.8-mile long, scenic road are no fewer than two low-water crossings and five cattle guards. This will bring you to the junc-tion with TX 27, where you turn right.

Follow TX 27 for 1.2 miles to FM 1350. Turn left, and in .2 mile plunge down to the Guada-lupe River. At this point you are 24.3 miles into the ride, so a thoroughly refreshing dip in the river might be fun—provided the season is ap-propriate.

Two miles further is the junction of FM 1350 and FM 480. The route turns left here, but for a historical side trip you may want to ride the three city blocks to the right to the town of Center Point. The old bank building with its in-teresting brick work was built in 1890 and Love's Store nearby was constructed in 1906. Turn around now and continue straight on FM 480 south.

One and one-half miles down this road is the first of three crossings of Verde Creek. Across the bridge on the right huge cypress trees line the bank of this creek flowing with the green water that gave it its Spanish name. FM 480 gently rolls along farm and ranch land with the cypress-lined banks of Verde Creek always nearby. At the junction with TX 173 turn right and cross Verde Creek again.

The Camp Verde store is a very interesting rest stop. The store itself was built in 1847. Near here, in 1857, the U.S. Army began a twelve year experiment with camels. Using camels and drivers from Egypt, the Army at-tempted to provide a superior means of trans-port for dry, western outposts. In 1869 the ex-periment was finally deemed a failure and abandoned. Very little of the original Camp Verde post remains today.

TX 173 rolls north for a pleasant 9-mile ride back to Kerrville State Park.

TOUR #3
Fredericksburg - Harper

ROUTE
TX 16 north - 24.4 miles
Fredericksburg City Tour - 5.0
  miles
TX 16 south - 2.2 miles
FM 2093 west - 22.6 miles
US 290 west - .4 mile
FM 783 south - 20.1 miles

DISTANCE
74.7 miles/119.5 kilometers

TERRAIN
Gently rolling to hilly

TRAFFIC
Light to none

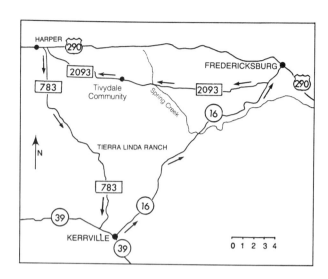

This farmhouse, built about 1846, can be seen on FM 783 on Tour #3.

Leaving Kerrville northbound on TX 16 there is a wide, smooth shoulder as far as the Kerr-Gillespie county line. From here, the road is a four-lane highway without dividing lines. This is essentially the same as having one lane and a shoulder. Past the county line, the road begins to climb to the two radio towers ahead. After this stiff climb is a long, terrific downhill. Your speed should carry you over some small humps and down again over Wolf Creek. From here the road pleasantly rolls the rest of the way into Fredericksburg.

From about 16 to 17 miles out of Kerrville to Fredericksburg you will see example after fine example of farmhouses built between 1860 and 1890. Constructed from local limestone blocks (as milled lumber was not available in this area until the turn of the century), these houses are quite fascinating in their design. Many farms have outside stairs which lead to a sleeping loft used by the children.

TX 16 will pass FM 2093 (also the airport road) and lead 2.2 miles further into Fredericksburg. At the junction of TX 16 with US 290, turn left and ride two blocks to the Pioneer Museum, a circular building on the right. Next

door is the chamber of commerce. Begin your city tour from here.

When you have finished touring Fredericksburg, go south on TX 16 for 2.2 miles to the airport road, FM 2093, and turn right. The rest of this tour, some 43 miles, best displays the character of the western hill country with mesquite, scrub oak, and cedar trees trying to survive in parched, limestone ground. Deer are in sufficient abundance that it is not unusual to see them in mid-afternoon, even on hot days.

On FM 2093, about 6.5 miles past the airport is a crossing over Spring Creek, which is a ma-

This old nineteenth century bank is only one of dozens of historic structures that can be seen on the Fredericksburg city tour.

Rest and drink up to prepare for the 20-plus mile ride back to Kerrville.

From the restaurant, return east on US 290 to the junction of FM 783. Turn right (south); there is a historical marker on the left recounting some difficulties the settlers had had with the Indians. It gives you an idea why this area was not settled until the 1840s and later.

Now, settle in for a long, straight, rolling section. About 2 miles after the first curve is a small stream crossing as the road winds to the left. As you come around the curve, to your left will be an old stone farm house that was one of the first in the area, built around 1846. No one will get upset if you take a closer look; it is well worth it.

FM 783 continues rolling and winding until it reaches Tierra Linda Ranch. This large development (there is a small store here) gives you the illusion of being near Kerrville. Actually, Kerrville is 6 miles further ahead. As the road climbs and swoops through the hills, be doubly sure to keep one eye on the scenery. There are some gorgeous views all the way into Kerrville.

There is a nice plunge at this end of FM 783 in Kerrville that takes you to the final junction of the route. At the traffic light, turn left onto TX 39/TX 27, and follow it back to the center of town.

jor tributary of the Pedernales River. On a hot day it is a perfect place to cool down. Less than 5 miles further is what remains of Tivydale Community. At the sign on the right that reads "Texas Hills Sporting Range," behind you and to the right is an old two-story frame house that in its day, was a grand home. Today it is but a forgotten memory.

There is a complete absence of traffic on this road, so you will have the place all to yourself. The traffic is all north of this route on paralleling US 290.

This solitude is shattered at the junction with US 290 in Harper. Turn left and enter town. There is a nice restaurant in the center of town on the right as you ride in. "Town" might be a misleading term, since Harper stretches for only about five blocks on both sides of US 290. Traffic barely slows as it passes through. You will have no trouble finding your way around.

The ride from Fredericksburg to Hooper on FM 2093 is characterized by limestone outcroppings and open range land. Livestock as well as wildlife can be seen along the roadside.

TOUR #4
Lower Crabapple Road

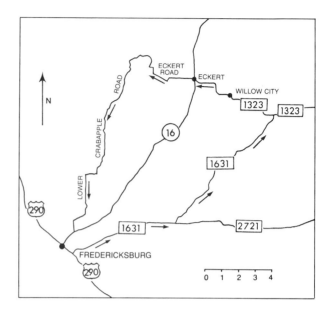

ROUTE
US 290 east - .6 miles
FM 1631 north - 16.8 miles
FM 1323 west - 6.1 miles
Eckert Road west - 5.0 miles
Lower Crabapple Road
   south - 11.4 miles
TX 16 south - 1.2 miles

DISTANCE
41.1 miles/65.8 kilometers

TERRAIN
Gently rolling to rolling

TRAFFIC
Nil

Although numerous books have already been written about the German heritage of Fredericksburg, one nice book by Joan Hubbard titled *Fredericksburg Self-Guiding Auto Tour*, is very convenient for the cyclist. It sells for two bucks, and contains photographs and descriptions of all the historic places you should visit, along with an easy-to-read map of the tour. The tour is about 5 miles round-trip and a "must" for the cyclist. The book can be purchased from the chamber of commerce or one of the numerous shops along Main Street.

Tour #4 begins on Main Street (also called US 290) in Fredericksburg. At the intersection of Main Street and TX 16 is the county courthouse. Park your car behind it and begin the ride here. Start east on Main, and continue to the junction with FM 1631. Turn left here and almost immediately, you are out of town.

The first two sections of this route combine to make a pleasant ride in the country. There are no difficult hills to climb, just rolling scenery that floats by almost surrealistically. You ride and ride and ride and still don't reach Willow City. But the ride is so enjoyable, you don't notice the time. Large limestone outcroppings,

expensive ranches, countless deer, and innumerable small creeks are all part of this pleasant Hill Country milieu. When you finally do reach the junction with FM 1323, you still have 3.4 miles to go to Willow City.

After a break in Willow City, continue on FM 1323 to the junction with TX 16. Here, you will make a right-then-left dogleg.

Immediately after turning right (north) onto TX 16, a small road leads to the left. This is Eckert Road. The road sign is hard to find, but there will be a large tree at the junction and a sign for Radke's Deer Processing.

If you thought the first half of this tour was great, you will think that this one-lane, paved trail was laid out with cyclists in mind. The road winds and climbs and plunges, and if you do not see deer along this half of the tour, you are not looking!

After a series of sharp right-left-right turns and a crossing of a cattleguard, you will come to Radke's Deer Processing. Take a sharp turn to the left and go up the driveway. Here you will find a store with soft drinks and the best smoked turkey sandwich in Texas. Even if you are not hungry now, you should get one to go, because it is a genuine Texas treat. Fresh water is also available, so fill up; it's a dry ride back into town.

Shortly after leaving Radke's, there is a "T" intersection. This is Lower Crabapple Road. Turn left here, and keep a sharp eye out for the original source of that wonderful sandwich. Turkeys are most often seen either at or near waterholes, or 40–50 yards off the road, in the bush. On a rare occasion, they will be seen streaking across the roadway.

I first rode this route during the annual Easter Hill Country Tour. I predicted that my companions and I would not see a single car on this portion of the route. Although we saw no cars, we did come upon an eighteen-wheel cattle truck. In a show of the kind of hospitality found frequently in this area, the truck driver pulled off the road for *us* to pass! There is a long plunge downhill and a rollercoaster ride you will be able to coast. Then after another strenuous climb you will start to see the first signs of "civilization." Isn't it odd how we call rude drivers, polluted air and crowded streets "civilization." The memory of this ride will last a lifetime.

Burnet

Where to Stay

MOTELS

You can obtain the names and addresses of motels in Burnet by contacting the chamber of commerce. (See "Appendix" for chamber addresses.) During hunting season advance reservations will be necessary.

CAMPING

There are no camping facilities for tents in Burnet. However, hook-ups are available at the city park and another park on South US 281 near the airport. Contact the city hall for information on these sites.

The nearest tent camping is at Inks Lake State Park, 12.5 miles west of town on US 29 and Park Road P4.

What to See

FORT CROGHAN

Established as one of eight forts that stretched from the Rio Grande to the site of present-day Fort Worth. The US Army stationed its first troops here in 1848. Fort Croghan proper came into being in early 1849. As settlers moved westward, so did the army garrisons. In 1855, Fort Croghan was officially

abandoned, but was used until the 1870s by local frontier guards to ward off Indian raids.

In 1957, the Burnet County Historical Society purchased the only surviving stone building and 1.7 acres of land. This building known as the "powder house" was joined by three other locally historic structures. The Fort Croghan Museum is run jointly by the Burnet County Historical Commission and the Burnet County Heritage Society.

The fort is open from March to September, from 8:00 a.m. to 5:00 p.m. Monday, Thursday, Friday, and Saturday; and from 1:00 p.m. to 5:00 p.m. on Sundays. A small admission fee is charged.

THE COUNTY JAIL

The Burnet County Jail has been in continuous use since it was built in 1888. Many a desperado has ended his career here. Built of local limestone, it boasts foot-thick walls.

LONGHORN CAVERN STATE PARK

This cave became a state park in 1932 thanks to work done by the Civilian Conservation Corps, and it became a registered National Landmark in 1971. Long before it was officially recognized, however, the cave was home to

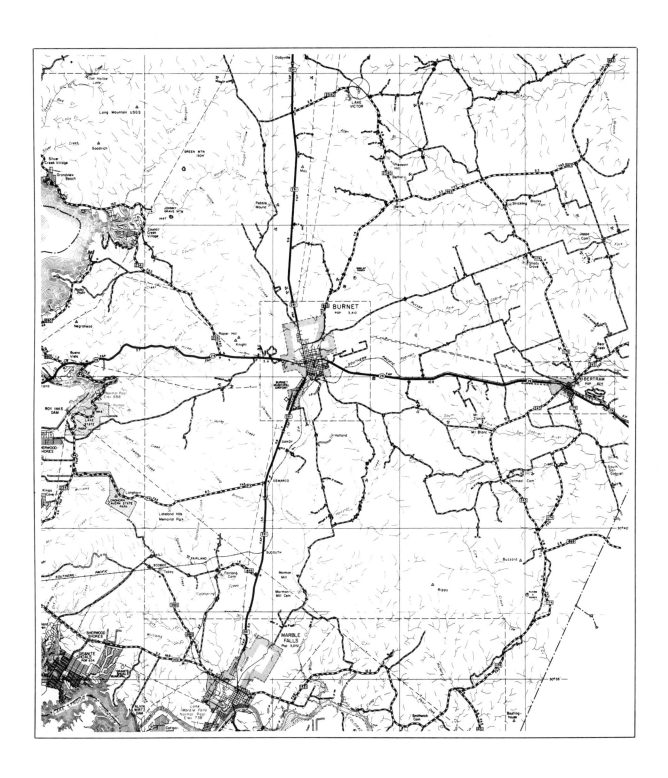

ancient dwellers. Their tools as well as some prehistoric fossils have been found there. The cave was also used as a stronghold for the Confederate Army during the Civil War, and after the turn of the century was a popular gathering place for area residents, as a dancehall, nightclub, and restaurant.

Tours lasting about an hour and a half are now conducted 1¼ miles through the cavern. The park also has a gift shop, snack bar, picnic area, and nature trails. Be sure to bring a sweater or light jacket, as the cave temperature stays a cool 64°F.

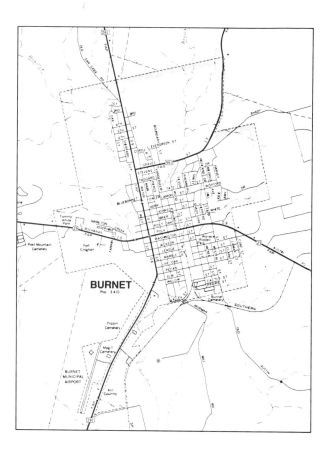

City Tour

The city of Burnet (pronounced burn-it) began with the establishment of Fort Croghan in 1848. The tour will begin at the most readily accessible location, the junction of US 281 (north and south) and US 29 (east and west).

Head west on US 28 for about one-half mile to Fort Croghan Drive. There is a sign that points the way at this intersection. A block off of US 29 are the grounds of Fort Croghan.

The infamous "Notch" on FM 1174 is the most difficult hill in the area, but the view from the top is fantastic.

From Fort Croghan, return to US 29 and turn right (east). At the intersection with US 281, continue straight for 1 block to Main Street. Turn right onto Main and one more block will take you into the town square. A ride around the square will reveal several historic buildings, including the old Masonic Lodge, one of the oldest original structures of Burnet remaining. Just off the northeast corner on Pierce Street is the county jail (ca. 1888).

Return to Main Street and ride south for 5 blocks to Elm Street. On the southwest corner is an original house dating back to the 1880s, with a market telling the story.

Continue on Main Street to the "T" intersection with Valley Street and turn left onto Valley. Follow Valley past Burnet Cemetery to McNeil Street, where you should turn left and ride to the "T" junction with League Street. Turn right and reenter the main square.

Although Burnet is a small, quiet town of some 4,300 people, it is in the heart of some of the most spectacular hill country scenery there is. In 1981, Burnet was officially recognized by the Texas State Legislature as the Bluebonnet Capital of Texas.

TOUR #1
Lake Victor

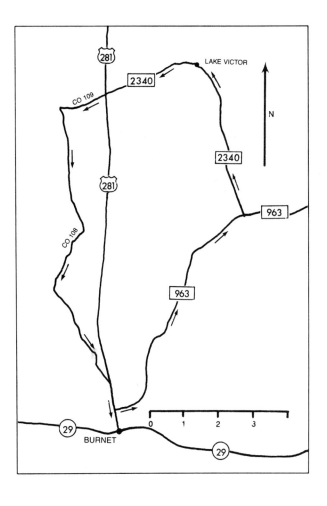

ROUTE
Us 281 north - .7 miles
FM 963 east - 7.9 miles
FM 2340 north - 7.6 miles
CO 109 west - 1.4 miles
CO 108 south - 9.8 miles
US 281 south - 1.4 miles

DISTANCE
28.1 miles/46.1 kilometers

TERRAIN
Gently rolling

TRAFFIC
Nil

"Gently rolling" is simply the best description of the entire tour. A gentle ride with gentle hills, this tour is excellent for the novice.

Take US 281 North to the turnoff to FM 963. Turn right and follow the main road out of town. The first section is predominantly up, but gently so.

As the road twists and climbs, the scenery behind you is often breathtaking. Also, through the entire tour, watch out for deer, turkeys, jackrabbits, road runners, and armadillos, all of which are common to the area.

The junction with FM 2340 is opposite the Bethel Church, one of many churches that seem to have been built in the middle of nowhere. Turn left onto FM 2340, and look back to your left at the panorama of farms and woods. It is really beautiful.

FM 2340 leads north for about five miles before curving west through the village of Lake Victor. Not only is there no lake, but, alas, no store. There are, however, some beautiful shade trees. Continue on FM 2340 to the intersection with US 281. At this point, cross the highway into the small paved road straight ahead, which is CO 109.

Follow CO 109 to the "T" junction with CO 108. Turn left (south) onto CO 108. This road is gentle, peaceful, and without a doubt offers the finest cycling in the area. Sit back, relax, go slow and watch for deer and other wildlife. Enjoy 9.8 of the best miles you'll ride anywhere. CO 108 brings you, sadly, back to US 281, where it is boring, busy, and bustling. Mercifully, it is only 1.4 miles back to the start.

If you start your ride at mid-afternoon and time your arrival at the junction of FM 2340 and US 281 to be about an hour and a half before sunset, the gentle ride along CO 108 and CO 109 will seem almost too good to be real. The view of the sunset and the glimpses of the wildlife that emerges then are well worth the effort of timing your ride.

TOUR #2
Longhorn Caverns State Park

ROUTE
TX 29 west - 2.0 miles
Hoover Valley Road south - 7.7 miles
Park Road P4 south - 9.7 miles
US 281 north - 4.9 miles

DISTANCE
24.3 miles/38.9 kilometers

TERRAIN
Gently rolling to hilly

TRAFFIC
Light to nil

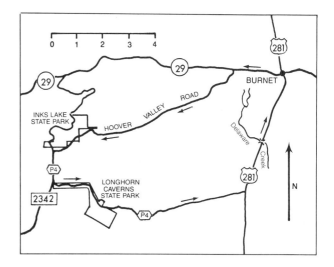

If you want the challenge of climbing a steep hill but feel one would be enough, this tour is for you.

Take US 29, westbound, for 2 miles to the sign that directs you to the left to Hoover Valley, along what is called, appropriately enough, Hoover Valley Road.

Roll and dip along this narrow road for a little less than 8 miles. Near the end, the road plunges into the southern portion of Inks Lake State Park. It is still four miles in the opposite direction of this tour to the park headquarters.

At the junction with Park Road P4, turn left (south). In a short distance, the road will "Y" with Park Road P4 bearing left and FM 2342 going right. Stay on Park Road P4 to the left.

You had better be prepared, with your toe straps tight, because the next two miles will be an exercise in deep breathing and thigh screaming. During this little ordeal, keep glancing to your right. This is what you are working for—an increasingly spectacular view. You may have to take several breaks on your

way up, and you will have just enough time to catch your breath before you pull into Longhorn Caverns State Park Headquarters. There is plenty of ice water and cold drinks at the fountain inside. You may appear a bit more disheveled than the other tourists who drove their cars up the hill, but your appearance will be forgotten as they marvel at your accomplishment.

If you plan to visit the cave proper, be sure to have a jacket along. The temperature inside the cave is a constant 64°F year-round. After that big climb and sweat, you'll freeze to death in the cave, so come prepared. A tour through the caverns is a must.

Now that you have rested and been refreshed and cooled, it's time for a few more light hills. Park Road P4 rolls along through classic Highland Lakes countryside before finally easing to a more gentle ride.

At the junction with US 281, turn left (north) and follow the smooth shoulder back to Burnet.

TOUR #3
Shady Grove Road—Bertram

ROUTE
US 281 north - .7 miles
FM 963 east - .7 miles
CO 200 east - 8.9 miles
FM 1174 south - 5.5 miles
FM 243 south - 3.5 miles
Mt Blanc Church Road West -
   8.5 miles

DISTANCE
27.8 miles/44.5 kilometers

TERRAIN
Gently rolling

TRAFFIC
Nil

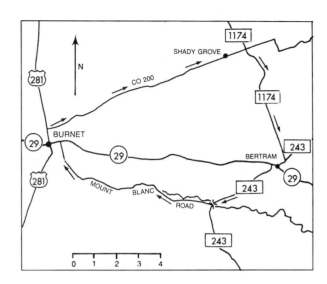

Not only does this tour share a common beginning with Tour #1, but also is similar with its narrow, empty country roads, an occasional panorama, and numerous deer, road runners, and other forms of native Texas wildlife.

As with Tour #1, start northbound on US 281 to the junction of FM 963. Turn right (east) onto FM 963. About three-quarters of a mile down the road, FM 963 curves to the left. A narrow, nondescript paved road leads "straight" off the curve. The signs are a little worn and vague, but this is Shady Grove Road or CO 200.

The county road system in Burnet County may be one of the best in the state. While in the area cycling, use the county map for some creative touring of your own. The county fathers probably had no idea what they did for cyclists, but you should take advantage of the wonderful "bike trails" they created.

At the end of CO 200 is the Shady Grove Church. The cemetery is a short distance down the paved road beside the church, and there is a historical marker at the church.

Within sight of the church is the junction with FM 1174. After your nearly nine miles on the narrow county road, FM 1174 will look big.

It still offers some pleasant surprises of its own, such as the crossing of the Russell Fork of the San Gabriel River. The low-water crossing earlier on CO 200 was also across this fork. Discovering the names of these creeks and streams will give you almost as much pleasure as crossing them will. There are the Cow, Honey, Dry, and Oatmeal creeks along with such streams as the Hickey Branch and Olive Branch. The pioneers must have had a field day thinking of what to call them all.

FM 1174 joins FM 243 at the edge of the Bertram city limits. Turn right (south) onto FM 243 into town.

Bertram is typical of so many small towns in Texas. The old homes and businesses built when Bertram was new are still there. One of the most famous and historic businesses is on TX 29—the A.B. McGill and Co. General Store (ca. 1860s). Built of local limestone, it stands as a reminder of a bygone era when one store would provide all the needs of area ranchers. A ride around Bertram to see the old structures is worth the time.

FM 243 jogs right onto TX 29 for a few blocks, then left again. The junctions are clearly marked.

The next turn on this tour is not so clearly marked. If you miss it, you might be lost forever . . . well, not quite, but watch carefully for it anyway. FM 243 makes a sweeping left curve 3.5 miles out of Bertram. About halfway through this curve is a church and a paved road on the right. The church is the Mount Blanc Church. That little lane beside the church is the road to take. Turn right. (You can't go wrong on this, it's the only way it goes!) From the Burnet end of this road, it is known as the Old Austin Road. But since you must find it with the aid of the Mount Blanc Church, I have dubbed it the Mount Blanc Road.

One more time, sit back and enjoy the peacefulness of this near-perfect cycling path. Mount Blanc Road will lead you directly into Burnet. Once in town, take any residential street back to US 29 or US 281.

TOUR #4
Marble Falls - "The Notch"

ROUTE
   Morman Mill Road south - 14.8
      miles
   US 281 south - .3 miles
   FM 1431 east - 12.5 miles
   FM 1174 north - 7.8 miles
   FM 243 north - 4.6 miles
   Mount Blanc Road west - 8.5
      miles

DISTANCE
   48.5 miles/77.6 kilometers

TERRAIN
   Gently rolling to hilly

TRAFFIC
   Moderate to nil

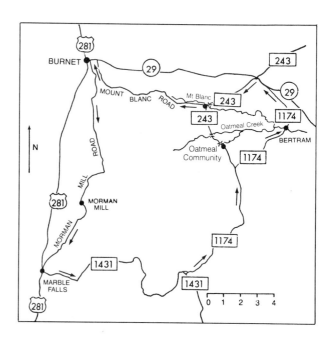

This tour is tough, and not recommended for the faint of heart or thigh. The middle third of this tour is very hilly, but what a challenge it is! Offering some spectacular views of Lake Marble Falls and the Highland Lakes scenery, it's worth the effort. Begin on Main Street at the town square. Follow Main Street south to the historic house on the corner of Elm Street, described in the Burnet city tour. Continue south on Main Street to the dead end at Valley Street and turn left onto Valley. Ride three blocks to the junction where the railroad tracks cross overhead. Turn right onto the small road that crosses under the two tressels. *Caution;* This part of the road is rough and may have loose gravel. There is no road sign, but the road you are now on is called Morman Mill Road. It leads first southeast and within one mile will curve sharply south.

Morman Mill Road is a narrow, but rider-friendly road with few hills and no traffic. The original location of Morman Mill is 9.3 miles from the railroad tracks. After the third low-water crossing the road turns sharply to the right, and 2.3 miles further is the location of the former mill. The land is now privately owned and closed to the public, but if someone is at the picnic area, ask permission to visit the beautiful pool and waterfall. It is beautiful. The creek that flows through here is Hamilton

Creek. Just ahead is a low-water crossing on the creek that reveals the subtle splendor of the area.

When you reach the city limits of Marble Falls, it is still two miles to US 281, and traffic will begin to pick up steadily.

Use extreme caution at the junctions with US 281 and FM 1431. If you wish to visit the center of Marble Falls, it is a great downhill plunge, but a huff-n-puff back to FM 1431. Have lunch here, rest, and be sure to get enough water. There is no water or food for the next 33.4 miles back to Burnet.

FM 1431 is best described as a rollercoaster road, with winding ups and twisting downs. The road offers some spectacular panoramas along the way, but it is still an arduous ride.

Even from a distance you will be able to see "the Notch," as you ride east on FM 1431. The Notch appears and disappears from view as the road winds through the hills. Finally you will reach the junction with FM 1174. Turn left (north) towards the Notch. From here you can see the road drop away and curve left out of sight only to reappear climbing sharply up to the Notch. You may be tempted at this point to hitchhike back to Marble Falls and take the bus to Burnet, but if serious cycling is what you came for, keep going—this is where it starts to get serious.

Gain as much momentum as you can on the downhill approach. As you begin the ascent, it will become necessary to drop to your lowest gear. Your thighs will scream in protest, but when you reach the top, the view is overwhelming.

At the top of the climb, on the right, is a small, paved road that leads up to the very top of the ridge and the edge of the escarpment. From this vantage point you will see the most amazing panorama in the entire area. It is truly worth that extra short climb. Be careful of the cattleguard, especially coming back down.

The next thing you will notice is there is no big downhill plunge on the other side. It is like being cheated out of half the prize for all the hard work it took to get there. FM 1174 leads through rolling terrain for the next half dozen miles and finally evens out to a pleasant, gentle roll. By now you are getting tired, thirsty, and hot and are wondering how much further it is to Burnet. This could make the lovely countryside seem less interesting.

FM 243 branches off of FM 1174 to the left (north) as FM 1174 curves to the right. The Mount Blanc Church is 4.6 miles further on FM 243. The church is marked by a white sign in front. It is the only structure in the immediate area. Next to the church is a small, paved lane with no name at this end. I have taken the liberty of dubbing it the Mount Blanc Road. On the Burnet end, the road is called the Old Austin Road.

Mount Blanc Road leads directly back into Burnet. The distance from the church to town is about 8.5 miles. Fortunately, the ride is much easier, the road much smoother, and the end is near. Don't be in too much of a rush to get to town, though, because this section is as nice to ride as was the first part of Morman Mill Road. Enjoy this last stretch; Burnet will arrive soon enough.

Section 2
Spot Tours

Kountze/Big Thicket

ROUTE

TX 326 south - .1 mile
FM 1293 west - 7.8 miles
FM 1003 north - 3.0 miles
FM 943 west - 22.3 miles
FM 2798 south - 10.8 miles
FM 787 east - 3.1 miles
FM 1293 north - 13.1 miles
FM 1003 north - 4.7 miles
FM 770 east - 4.5 miles
TX 326 north - 2.6 miles

DISTANCE

72.0 miles/115.2 kilometers

TERRAIN

Flat to gently rolling

TRAFFIC

Nil

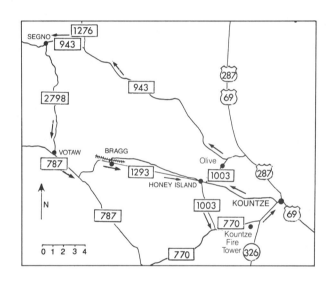

The Big Thicket, a large area of southeast Texas covered with dense pine and desiduous forest, is very aptly named. This tour is excellent for the novice who wants a long ride through a scenic area.

Kountze is located about 15 miles north of Beaumont on US 69/287. TX 326 turns south in the center of town and leads two blocks to the Hardin County Courthouse on the left. Park here and begin the tour.

From the courthouse parking lot, turn left onto TX 326. Go one block to the junction with FM 1293, and turn right. The next 7.5 miles have 7 bridges across creeks, which immediately introduce you to the thick jungle-like growth of the Big Thicket. The road is flat and closely crowded by forest.

The junction with FM 1003 is preceded by a sign indicating "JCT. US 69." You may want to go past this turn and visit the store which is .1 mile past in Honey Island since it is a long way to the next watering hole. Return to this junction and continue the tour by turning left on FM 1003. (Do not be confused by the "FM 1003" junction directly opposite the store in Honey Island. This junction comes later in the tour.) This short section on FM 1003 has quite a

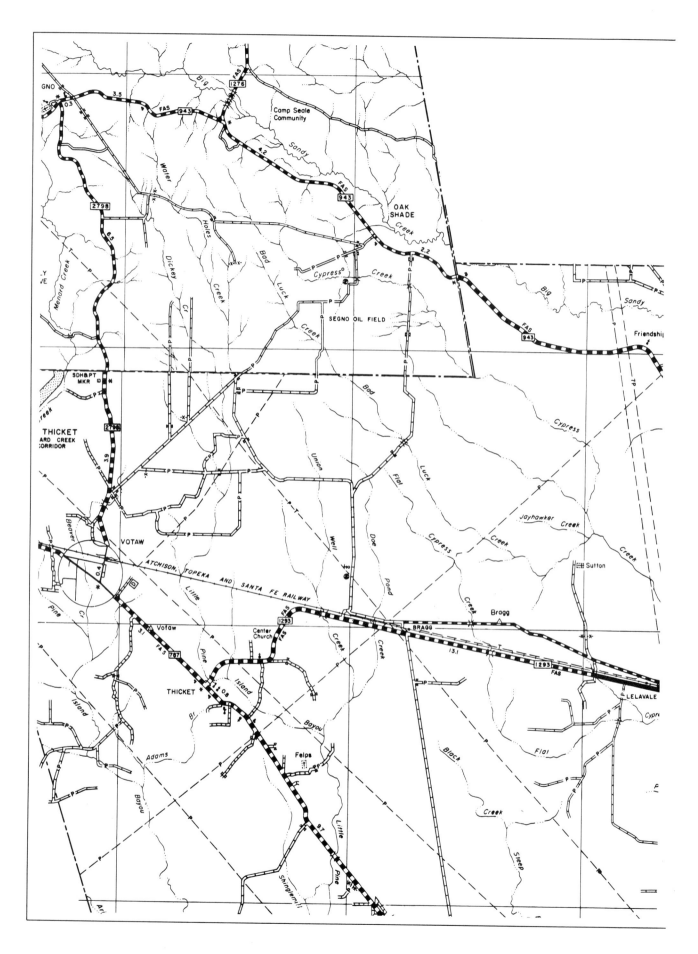

This swamp pond in the Big Thicket has an eerie ambience that can be enjoyed if you start your tour early in the morning.

few houses and several beer joints along it. At the junction with FM 963 turn left.

This long stretch is typical of the Big Thicket. The road is flat with high, dark forest walls on both sides. Occasionally, areas of pines have been harvested, leaving ragged stands of cottonwoods and other trees. At the county line, about 12 miles in, is a small beer joint and the forest closes back in on the road. The route becomes gently rolling through this section until you reach Segno. Bear left at the "Y" junction with FM 1276 and stay on FM 963. It is about 4 miles to Segno from this junction.

In Segno is the junction with FM 2798 and a much-welcomed store. Turn south onto FM 2798. This 11-mile section to Votaw has a rougher surface than usual, but it is nothing for concern.

At the stop sign in Votaw, turn left (east) onto FM 787 towards Saratoga. There is a store at this junction, also.

Three miles out of Votaw, turn left at the junction with FM 1293. This long, flat road will parallel the tracks of the Atchison, Topeka, and Santa Fe railroad.

The historical marker at Bragg offers an interesting diversion. The marker tells the story of the old townsite of Bragg, of which, nothing is left today. If you enjoy cycling in solitude take the small dirt road just past the sign that leads to the left, across the tracks. A paved road "T's" into the dirt road to the right, just across the tracks. Turn right onto this lane and follow it straight for 7 miles. It will recross the tracks and connect again with FM 1293 in Honey Island.

Regardless of which route you choose, you will arrive in Honey Island and at the general store. Take a break, then cross FM 1293 onto FM 1003 opposite the store.

Follow FM 1003 south to the "T" junction with FM 770. Turn left (east) onto FM 770. This section will take you past the Kountze Fire Tower. Across yet another bridge is the junction with TX 326. Turn left and follow this road back to the courthouse.

Glen Rose

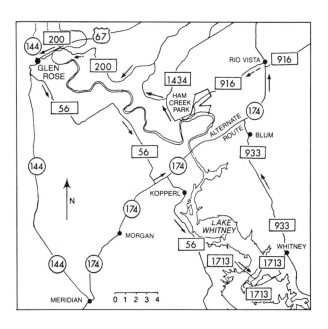

ROUTE
TX 144 south - .7 miles
FM 56 east - 17.5 miles
TX 174 east - 1.4 miles
FM 56 south - 10.7 miles
FM 1713 east - 10.0 miles
FM 933 north - 13.8 miles
TX 174 east - 5.6 miles
FM 916 west - 8.9 miles
Dirt road west/north - 4.8 miles
FM 1434 west - 5.7 miles
FM 200 west - 12.3 miles
US 67 west - 3.7 miles

DISTANCE
95.1 miles/152.2 kilometers

TERRAIN
Gently rolling to very rolling

TRAFFIC
Light to nil

This tour is the longest in the book and is not recommended for beginners. On this tour, you will find lots of hills, wind, gravel roads, and a long stretch without services. Carry extra water and something to eat—you will appreciate having it. If you have sew-up tires or old, bald clinchers, don't try it. But, if you have good tires, a strong bike, stronger legs and are not afraid of a little gravel, then this ride will be one to test your mettle.

The Glen Rose town square is located a couple of blocks south of US 67. Parking is available here. Signs on either end of town direct you downtown through residential streets. TX 144 leaves the square from the south corner. Follow this road out to the edge of town to the junction with FM 56. Turn left onto FM 56 and settle in for a long, rolling ride through some gorgeous scenery. FM 56 has numerous turns and curves and a surprising number of steep hills. It roughly follows the west side of the Brazos River.

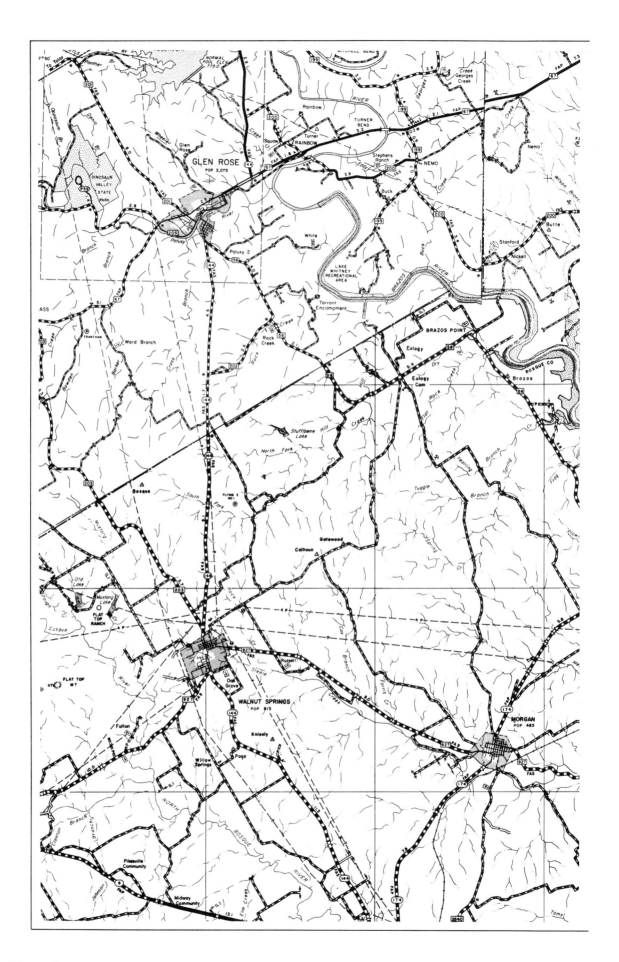

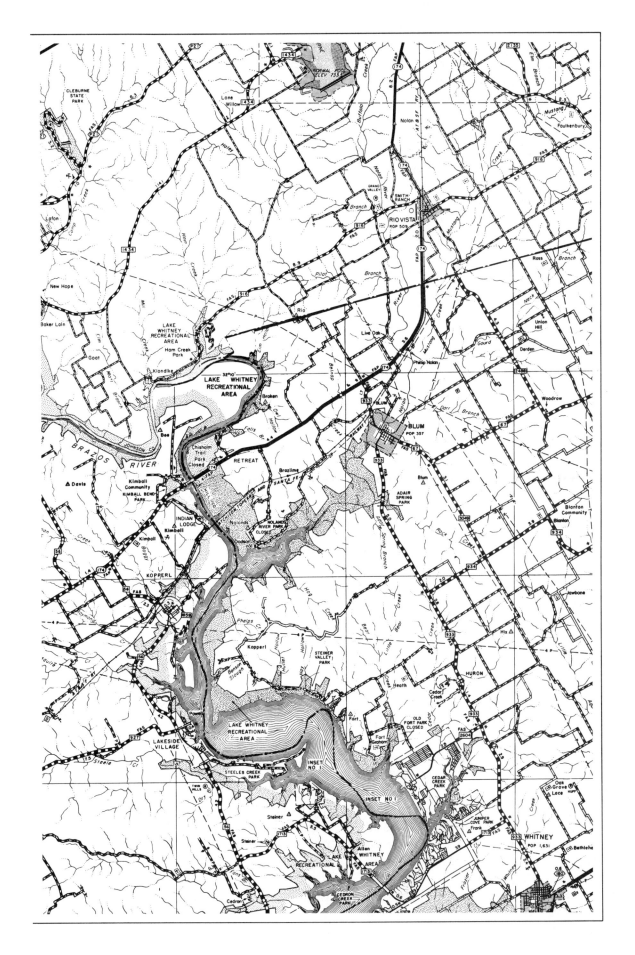

The first community on the route is Brazos Point. The store there is open sporadically, and you shouldn't depend on it for a snack stop. Riding south out of Brazos Point, you will cross several creeks that feed the Brazos River. There are also many more dips and whoop-dee-dos.

At the junction with TX 174, turn left. FM 56 continues with TX 174 for 1.4 miles before turning south again. Stay on FM 56 towards Kopperl. In Kopperl, the store is closed on Sunday, but water is available from a hose across the street. Be sure to fill up; it is about 15 miles to the next break.

Continue on FM 56 and watch to your left for glimpses of Lake Whitney in the distance. A few more miles of dips and hills will finally bring you to the junction of FM 1713 and the end of the section on FM 56. Turn left onto FM 1713.

The section will flatten out as you begin to approach the lake itself. About 5 miles past the turn onto FM 1713, you will reach the long bridge across the lake. If there is any wind, you will feel it here. A half-mile past the bridge, the road reaches a junction with another road also called FM 1713! Go left (east). At this junction, on your left, is a string of businesses. Among them is a cafe with good food that is an excellent spot for a lunch break.

Continue east on FM 1713 to the junction with FM 933. Turn left (north) and enjoy a mixture of rolling, curving, and straight road through pretty forest-covered hills like those seen at the beginning of the route. Eventually, you will reach the town of Blum. Stay on FM 933 through town, and it will bring you to the junction with TX 174.

At this junction, you have a choice. The gravel road is coming up shortly. If you absolutely, positively cannot face a gravel road for any distance or reason, then turn left onto TX 174. Follow it back to FM 56 north, and repeat the first leg of the route. It is 28.5 miles back to Glen Rose.

Personally, a little gravel doesn't bother me, but the thought of repeating a section I have already cycled does. That is why I have designed these tours as "loops." So if you are still with me, turn right onto TX 174 towards Rio Vista. This section will usually have some light traffic, but there is plenty of room for bikes, too. It is also a short section—just over five miles to

Lake Whitney is one of Texas' most popular recreation areas and provides a convenient place for a refreshing dip.

the next junction. *Caution!* Be sure to get plenty of water and food in Rio Vista. There will be nothing for the next 30-plus miles back to Glen Rose.

TX 174 leads straight through Rio Vista. At the north end, it takes a bend to the left and in this bend is the junction with FM 916. Turn left (west) and follow this pleasant road for some 9 miles to Ham Creek Park in the Lake Whitney Recreational Area. This is actually on the Brazos River and not the lake proper. At the end of FM 916, the gravel road begins. Continue straight on this road (there is no place to turn off along the first part). It seems farther than it really is to the next turn. This turn is signalled by a short but steep climb. You will *know* the hill when you reach it. Stay out of the loose stuff, or you won't make it up. The road will make another bend to the left and become almost flat and straight. Turn right onto the first road that "T's" into the road you are on. This right turn is, in fact, the *first* right turn you can make from the end of the pavement. As I mentioned before, it seems farther than it really is. The distance from end-of-pavement to the right turn is 2.1 miles. The road to the right is obvious and once you are on it, the riding becomes much easier. This road is about 2.7 miles long and offers some beautiful scenery of pleasant, rolling farm land. At the end is a long, winding downhill that is not too steep, but requires some caution. At the end, around a corner, is the unmarked junction with FM 1434. There is no way to miss this junction—it is the first paved road you come to (and a welcome sight it is, too!). Turn left (west) onto FM 1434.

This section traces a "horseshoe" swing from west to north to east and curves back north again. It is a very relaxing ride after the last gravel sections.

By the time you reach the junction of FM 1434 and FM 200, you may be pretty tired, but you still have a good ways to go.

Turn left onto FM 200 and this rolling, scenic road will lead most of the way back to Glen Rose. The scenery along this section is worth paying attention to, so try not to let your fatigue interfere with your viewing pleasure. In the little town of Nemo, there is only a post office. No food is available, but it is only 3.9 miles more to a soft drink machine. FM 200 makes a left turn into Nemo and rolls and winds to another crossing of the Brazos River. Just past the bridge and before the junction with US 67, is a small road that leads to the left. There is a soft drink machine on the northwest corner of this intersection. Though this information may seem unimportant now, it will be invaluable when you reach this point.

The little road you are on parallels US 67 into Glen Rose. The pavement is a little rough, but it beats the traffic on US 67. Follow it back to

This cyclist is experiencing the best in Texas cycling—a level, little-traveled road, nice weather, and a close-up view of the myriad Texas wildflowers. What more could anyone ask for?

Glen Rose. When you reach the square, congratulate yourself—you have just completed one tough century.

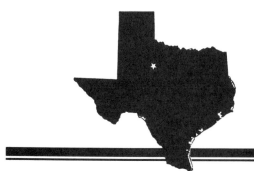

Spur

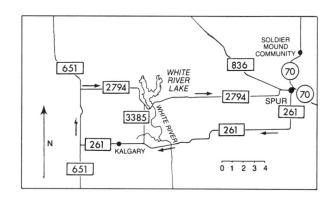

ROUTE
FM 261 south - 24.4 miles
FM 651 north - 5.1 miles
FM 2794 east - 22.5 miles

DISTANCE
52.0 miles/83.2 kilometers

TERRAIN
Flat to rolling

TRAFFIC
Nil

Spur is roughly located west of the Croton Breaks, east of White River, south of Soldier Mound and north of nowhere. The town is a clone of any number of towns in the Panhandle, and all have areas worth cycling. I chose Spur, because it is a nice ride.

TX 70 cuts across the north and west edges of town. You will need to drive into the downtown area, and park anywhere along the main business section. Signs will direct you to FM 261, heading south. Start the tour on this road.

FM 261 starts out flat for a good distance. About 3.5 miles south of town, it makes an abrupt right turn and continues flat. You can clearly see the Caprock Escarpment ahead, and *this* is what the ride is all about. The route begins to climb and wind around. Not only does the terrain change, but also, you discover there are trees in the Panhandle. After crossing White River, the road wiggles around some more before straightening and flattening out. There is a wide spot along the road called Kalgary, but there are no services here. Three miles farther is the junction with FM 651 where you should turn right (north).

This short section has several small creek crossings, which are always a pleasant diversion, and one bridge over McDonald Creek.

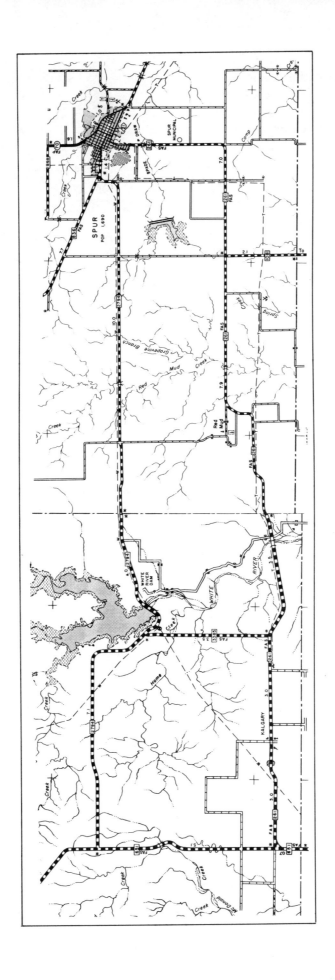

The next junction with FM 651 is FM 2794. Turn right (east) and enjoy the gentle ride and low rolling hills capped with forests. As you approach White River Lake, the road will begin to roll and dip down the escarpment again. White River Dam is a marina-style community with limited services available. The route will cross the dam itself and whoop-de-do around some more before finally leveling off. FM 2794 will become straight for about 10 miles, then has a series of sharp left-right turns. It meets FM 836 angling in from the left, and together, they will bring you back into Spur.

It is a simple ride, but is worth the time if you happen to be in the area.

You might miss this surprising sight if you were speeding along in your car, but on bicycle you have plenty of time to take in all the flora and fauna along your route. You might even see a bison such as this one near Navasota.

Palo Duro Canyon
State Park

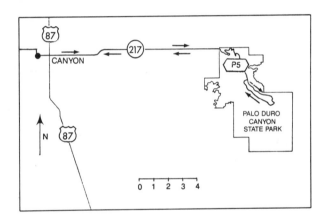

ROUTE
TX 217 east - 11.4 miles
Park Road P5 (round trip) - 20.6
   miles
TX 217 west - 11.4 miles

DISTANCE
43.4 miles/69.5 kilometers

TERRAIN
Flat, except for Canyon Rim
   Section

TRAFFIC
Light to nil

Canyon is a quiet little college town a few miles south of Amarillo. If you are coming from Amarillo, you may wonder where there could be any pleasant place to cycle in the area. The terrain can only be described as *flat,* and there is also the ever-present wind. Riding a long, straight, flat road into gusts of 20-30 mph does not sound pleasant. However, the best kept secret in all of Texas is Palo Duro Canyon. It is truly a wonder of nature. Second in size to

that other hole out west, it is 120 miles long and 20 miles wide in places.

Starting at the junction of US 87 and TX 217, ride east on TX 217. No matter which way the wind is blowing, it always seems to be in your face, but it is only 11.4 miles to the canyon rim, and the ride is tolerable. The destination, of course, would make *almost* anything tolerable.

Just before the entrance to the park, on the right, is a campground/store/cafe. Behind the store and to the right is a dirt road that leads to the campsites. Follow this road to the edge of the canyon and prepare yourself for a breath-taking view. From this vantage point, you are over 350 feet above the floor of the canyon. Down the canyon to the east, on the south

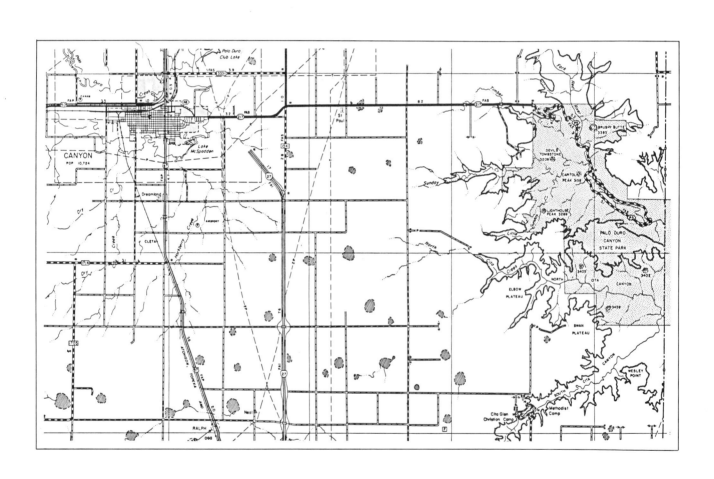

side, is a multi-colored layering of rock and scree. This formation is called a Mexican skirt. It is made up of yellow, red, and purple bands that are brilliantly highlighted in the setting sun.

Return to the highway and enter the park. Stop at the park entrance headquarters and inquire about road conditions in the park! If it has been raining recently, the road may be flooded. Pick up a map, also. It will show the locations and names of the various formations in the canyon, such as Devil's Tombstone, Brushy Butte, and Capitol Peak.

The plunge down the rim is incredible. Hairpin turns add to the challenge of your skills. Five winding miles into the park, the road splits into a five-mile loop. This loop is much more straight and flat than the first half. By the time you have completed this loop, you will agree, Palo Duro Canyon *is* the best kept secret in Texas.

Of course, now that you have had your fun coming down into the canyon, you have to climb back *up* to the rim. The climb is arduous and once you are on top, flat ground will never

The Palo Duro Canyon is a surprisingly beautiful interruption in the flat and empty landscape of the Texas Panhandle.

have looked so good. Take a well-earned break at the cafe. When you are well fed and rested, get ready for the ride back to Canyon. The wind will probably have swung around into your face again.

Buffalo Lake National Wildlife Refuge

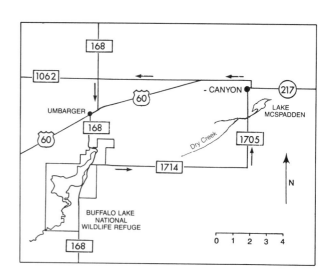

ROUTE

TX 217 west/north - 1.5 miles
US 60 west - 3.5 miles
FM 1062 west - 5.9 miles
FM 168 south - 1.9 miles
US 60 west - .6 miles
FM 168 south - 2.0 miles
Buffalo Lake National Wildlife
   Refuge - 2.0 miles
FM 168 east - 1.4 miles
FM 1714 east - 9.4 miles
Unnamed, paved road,
   north - 4.8 miles

DISTANCE

33 miles/52.8 kilometers

TERRAIN

Flat

TRAFFIC

Nil to moderate on US 60

This route looks far more complicated than it really is. It is roughly a rectangle with Canyon and Buffalo Lake National Wildlife Refuge on opposite corners.

Beginning at the junction of TX 217 and US 87 in Canyon, ride west on 217. Follow it through town as it turns north, crosses the railroad tracks, and connects with US 60.

Turn left onto US 60 and endure the traffic here for 3.5 miles to the cut-off on FM 1062. Once you are on FM 1062, the ride gets easier. Relax and hope for a tail wind.

At the junction with FM 168, turn left (south) and reconnect with US 60. Fortunately, US 60 only lasts another .6 mile into Umbarger, where there are refreshments. Here also, FM 168 continues south to the Buffalo Lake wildlife refuge. Immediately past a 90-degree left turn on FM 168 is the entrance. Within the ref-

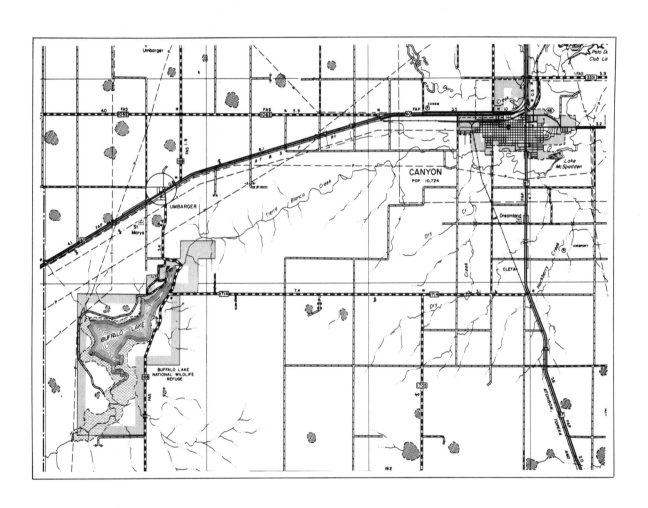

uge is a short loop that leads you through the marsh and along the lake shore. The refuge is home to numerous migratory birds including several species of ducks and the Canadian goose. Other types of marsh birds and animals abound. This is a birdwatcher's paradise, and a great place to snap pictures.

Continuing on FM 168 for another winding mile and a half, turn left onto FM 1714. This section is 9.4 miles *straight* east. "Straight" and "flat" are the key features of Panhandle cycling. You will ride past fields of wheat, soy, sorghum, alfalfa, and hay, and at 7.4 miles pass the junction with FM 1705. Continue on FM 1714 for another 1.3 miles to the bridge over Dry Creek. Though the bridge is somewhat nondescript, it is the signal for the next turn off, which is the next paved road to the left .7 mile past the bridge. This little road leads *straight* back north into Canyon.

This is an easy ride for all levels, if the wind is accommodating.

One of the advantages of touring by bicycle is the ease with which you can stop and examine interesting sights along the way more closely. A restored log cabin is just one of the many historic or scenic views awaiting the cyclist who takes one of the tours included here. This cabin is on TX 21 near the Attoyac Bayou crossing.

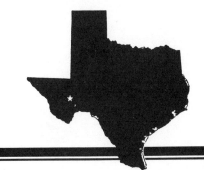

Fort Davis

ROUTE
TX 17 north - 1.4 miles
TX 118 west - 28.1 miles
TX 166 south - 43.0 miles
TX 17 north - 2.3 miles

DISTANCE
73.8 miles/118.1 kilometers

TERRAIN
Mountainous to flat

TRAFFIC
Nil

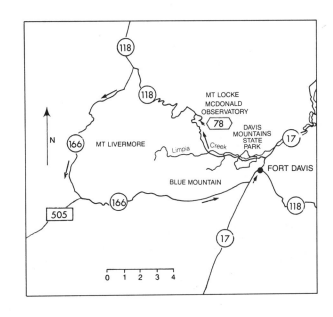

This is the most spectacular ride in Texas. Period. Known as the scenic loop, this tour has nearly everything to offer the cyclist—the highest road in Texas (at 6,791 feet), the longest stretch continuously above 5,280 feet elevation (34 miles), the steepest grade, on Mount Locke (with a maximum grade of 17%), the simplest route to follow (only three left turns), and the widest variety of terrain (beginning in the mountains, cutting through rolling valleys and ending in flat, open rangeland).

Fort Davis is much more than "just another spectacular ride." Located in the Davis Mountains, which has surrounding peaks up to 8,382 feet high, Fort Davis was originally an Army outpost. The original fort was established in 1854 and remained active until 1891. It was home to the first black regiments and the first black graduate of West Point. Today, Fort Davis National Historic Site is at the north end of town on TX 17.

In downtown Fort Davis is the Limpia Hotel, built in 1912. The original structure contains nine rooms upstairs and two suites on the first floor. A new complex has been added with eight more rooms and full hotel facilities. There are two other motels in Fort Davis. Other accommodations in the area include

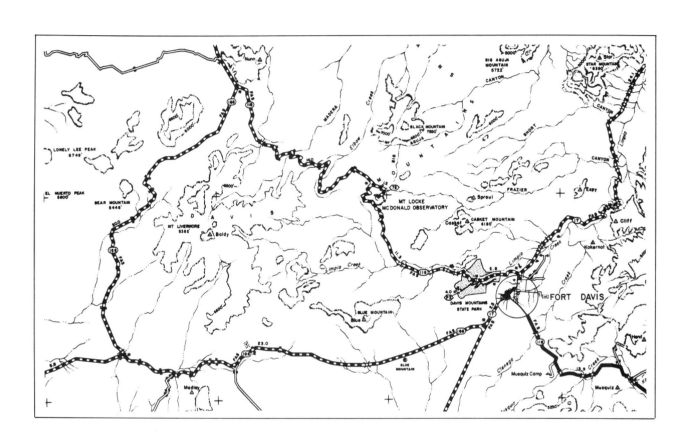

Davis Mountain State Park and the Prude Ranch.

Davis Mountain State Park has full camping facilities and the historic Indian Lodge (ca. 1933). The park is located 4 miles out of town on TX 118. If the Scenic Loop hasn't exhausted you, take a ride up the Skyline Drive in the evening. The view is indescribable. The two scenic overlooks are nearly 6,000 feet in elevation.

The Prude Ranch is a dude ranch open to the public. It has full motel and bunkhouse facilities, as well as swimming, horseback riding, and trail hiking. There are areas for tent camping as well. The Prude Ranch is located 5 miles from Fort Davis on TX 118.

Back in Fort Davis are three museums: The Overland Trail Museum (ca. 1833), The Neill Museum (ca. 1898), and The Museum of Natural History of the Davis Mountains. As you can see, Fort Davis is steeped in history, and there is much to discover for yourself in this rich area.

To begin your ride, start north from the Jeff Davis County Courthouse on TX 17 past the main shopping strip. On the left, you will pass the Fort Davis National Historic Site. The road will then drop to the junction with TX 118. Turn left. A sign on the right will announce the Scenic Loop. On the left is a small ruin and historical marker. This was the pumphouse for Old Fort Davis. The creek on the right is Limpia Creek, and you will be ascending Limpia Canyon for a few miles. Further along the route is a short, stiff climb to the entrance of Davis Mountain State Park. From this vantage point, you can see McDonald Observatory to your right above an intervening ridge. If your legs and lungs hold out, that's where you will be shortly.

Continuing on TX 118, a mile or so farther you will pass the entrance to the Prude Ranch on the right. From this point, the *serious* climbing will begin.

A suggestion: At the top of each climb, rest. Get off the bike and sit on the guardrail, take deep breaths, and survey the scenery. It took me *nine hours* for the entire trip, including all the time visiting the observatory and gasping for breath after each climb. In short, take your time and enjoy the ride.

The McDonald Observatory is one of the man-made points of interest in the beautiful Davis Mountains.

As the route winds up the mountains, you will have several views of McDonald Observatory. A sign around a steep curve will announce the 6,000-foot level and just ahead is the visitor center for the observatory. Stop here for two reasons: First, you will need to refill your water bottles. It's 50-plus miles with no more water to Fort Davis. Second, you will need to rest and *then* decide if you want to try the 17% grade up to the top of Mount Locke. If you don't try, you will forever regret it. If you do make it, you will have a sense of accomplishment unmatchable in Texas cycling. It's only about fifteen minutes up and a minute back down. The summit of Mount Locke is 6,791 feet, the highest paved road in the state.

Don't forget water! Whether you try the ride to the summit or not, you will continue the rest of the trip from the visitor center. The route will continue winding with steep ups and downs. Five-and-a-half miles past the visitor center is a very dangerous hairpin curve. The road plunges down to the right and at the bot-

Panoramic vistas such as this one are one of the many rewards gained from some strenuous hill climbing in the Davis Mountains.

tom of the hill is a sharp, left turn. Overestimate this curve and you will end up in the gravel.

After this little adventure, the route will drop into Madera Canyon with its pine-shaded picnic area. Thrilling views will open to the left of Mount Livermore (8,382 feet) and Sawtooth Mountain (7,718 feet). In the shadow of Sawtooth Mountain is the Rockpile. This was once open to the public for picnicking and exploring, but vandalism has forced the closing to help preserve the remaining Indian pictographs.

A long downhill whoosh will bring you to the junction with TX 166. Turn left here. Suddenly, the road looks easier and the mountains fall away behind you. From here it is twenty miles of rolling to gently rolling terrain populated by bison, deer (both white tail and mule), and pronghorn antelope.

There is a junction "in the middle of nowhere" with FM 505. Continue on TX 166 and it will lead into a wonderful canyon area. For several miles, the route winds through this peaceful scenery. Here, you will forget the pain of the climbs and begin to realize how spectacular and sublime this tour is.

Skillman Grove, the next point of interest, is the home of Bloys Camp Meeting. This old-fashioned cowboy camp has held interdenominational religious services each August for over 75 years.

The route finally evens out and flattens into a predominantly descending ride. Near the end of this memorable journey is the Point of Rocks picnic area. It is located at the base of Blue Mountain (7,330 feet), and you will find it is aptly named because of the enormous cascade of boulders.

A few miles more is the junction with TX 17. Turn left and 2.3 miles later, the trip is over.

With its high passes, deep canyons, open range, and abundant wildlife, this tour will be long remembered.

Leakey

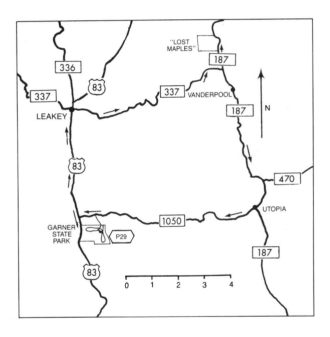

ROUTE
FM 337 east - 15.2 miles
FM 187 north - 1.0 miles
Lost Maples State Park
FM 187 south - 12.5 miles
FM 1050 west - 14.3 miles
US 83 south - 1.0 miles
Garner State Park US 83
   north - 8.7 miles

DISTANCE
53.1 miles/85 kilometers

TERRAIN
Flat to very hilly, almost
mountainous

TRAFFIC
Nil

This tour includes flat, peaceful roads, but the terrain that isn't flat is almost mountainous. If you want to test your mettle against the Hill Country, then this tour is for you.

You can start from either Garner or Lost Maples State Park or from Leakey. There is lodging in Leakey and camping at both state parks. Lost Maples State Park is particularly beautiful in late October when the leaves change color. For the sake of simplicity, the description of the tour will begin in Leakey.

Leakey is located on one of the least-traveled major highways in Texas, US 83. This highway runs from Brownsville to Canada! Unlike its busy counterpart, US 59 in East Texas, US 83 is mostly deserted through west central Texas and just right for cyclists.

Leakey is quite easy to find your way around in. It runs north/south along US 83, with the intersection with FM 337 at the center. Begin the tour here, eastbound on FM 337.

This road starts out innocently enough. It is a gentle climb up into the hills for the first part, but all of a sudden you come through a deep cut in the hill where the road plunges out of sight. The grade is about 8% with a slight right-hand curve at the bottom. If your downhill

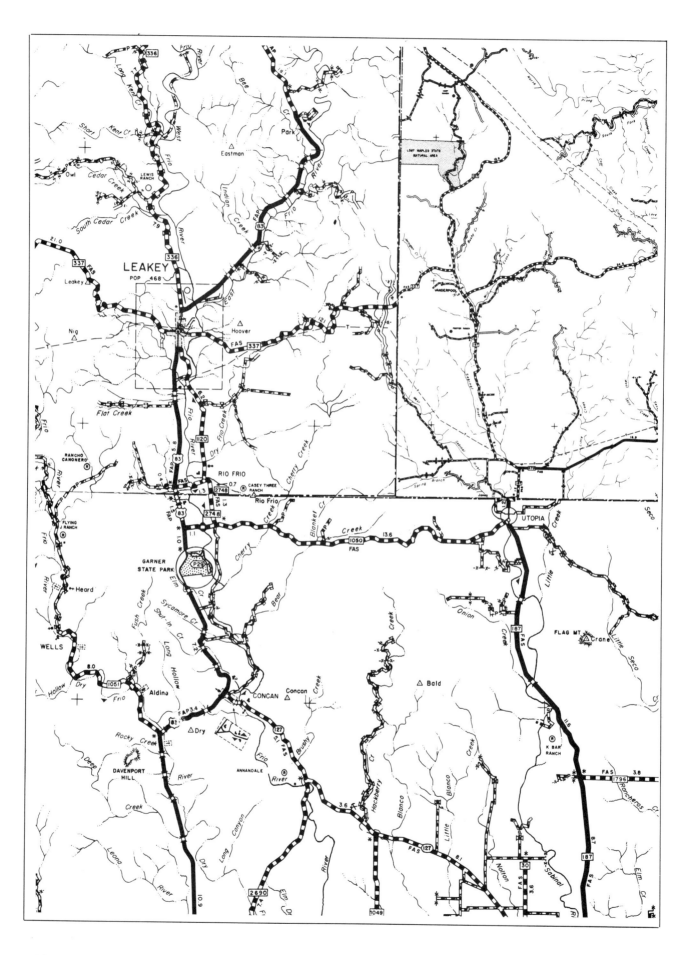

This rolling Hill Country landscape is typical of the kind of spectacular scenery found around Leakey.

skills are sharp, you can let go and make the curve. I don't recommend doing this, though, because the hill is very steep and your speed becomes too great.

Once you have survived the Big Plunge, the road begins a long, winding climb. Be sure to take the time to look to your left and back over your left shoulder. The scenery along here is as grand as any in the Hill Country. This climb is long and tough, so make sure your granny gears are well oiled. Once you regain the top, the climbing eases and the terrain becomes rolling. All your efforts are rewarded with a nice downhill ride to the junction with FM 187.

There is also a store on the left at this junction, a most welcome sight.

To the left is Lost Maples State Park. If you are a real glutton for pain, continue north past the state park and climb the next double-hill. This little treat is about a mile-and-a-half long and a 12% maximum grade. When you reach the top, turn around and fly back down.

After a restful visit to Lost Maples, return south on FM 187 past the store and on into Vanderpool. The road now is gently rolling to flat as you parallel the Sabinal River and a marked change from the first section. There are many trees along the river and several crossings as both road and river wind through the valley. This 12.5 mile stretch is absolutely relaxing. You may even opt for a swim in the river at one of the crossings. The setting will seem like Utopia!

In fact, Utopia is the next town, and there you turn right (west) at the junction with FM 1050. Immediately after the turn is yet another crossing of the Sabinal River and another chance for a refreshing dip before the upcoming hill climbing. The road dips and plunges for a series of rolling hills and spectacular views. At the top of each hill be sure to look back.

There is a final downhill run to a low-water crossing of the Frio River, and then the junction with US 83. Turn south onto US 83 to Garner State Park. After your vigorous ride, a swim in the Frio River will be as exhilarating as your dip in the Sabinal before the hills. You can take it easy for the next 9 miles of gently rolling road back to Leakey and the end of this well-rounded trip. For scenery, challenging riding, and pleasant rest stops, this trip can't be beat.

Section 3
Inter-City Tours

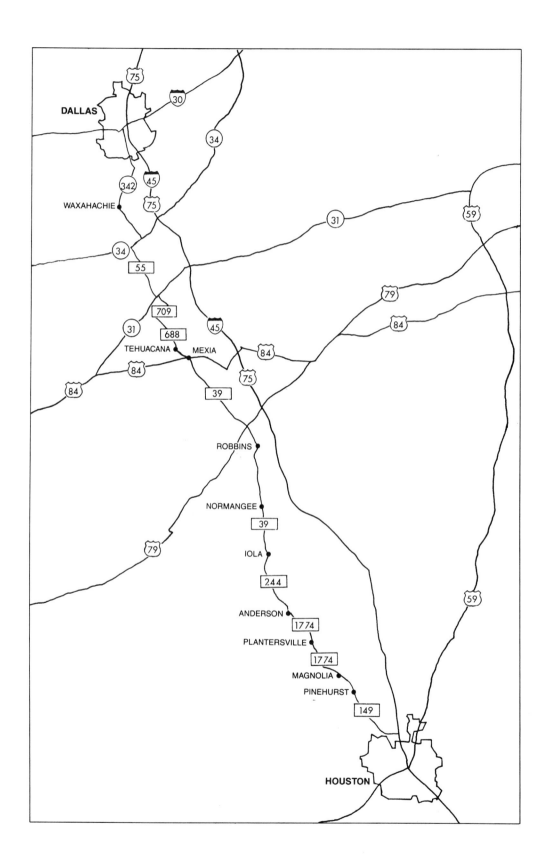

Dallas to Houston

ROUTE
TX 342 south - 22.0 miles
US 77 south to Waxahachie - 7.1 miles
Follow US 77 through town, cross railroad tracks to junction - .3 miles
FM 877 east - 13.1 miles
TX 34 west to Avalon - 4.4 miles
FM 55 south - 24.0 miles
FM 709 west - 4.0 miles
FM 638 south to Tehuacana - 14.0 miles
TX 171 south to Mexia - 6.0 miles
FM 39 south to Iola - 72.0 miles
FM 244 south - 21.0 miles
TX 90 south to Anderson - 2.0 miles
FM 149 east - 1.0 mile
FM 1774 south to Pinehurst - 33.0 miles
FM 149 south to Houston - 38.0 miles

DISTANCE
261.9 miles/419.1 kilometers

TERRAIN
Mostly flat to gently rolling

TRAFFIC
Mostly light to nil. South of Magnolia on FM 1774, traffic increases exponentially as you approach Houston. Cycling in Houston is dangerous to say the least.

The only part of this ride that might confuse you is after you reach Waxahachie. Follow US 77 through town and across the railroad tracks and Waxahachie Creek. The next junction is a multiple one, with several roads coming together. At the stop light, turn left onto FM 877. This road takes you past Lake Waxahachie and will connect with TX 34. Turn right onto TX 34. The rest of the route is on the state map.

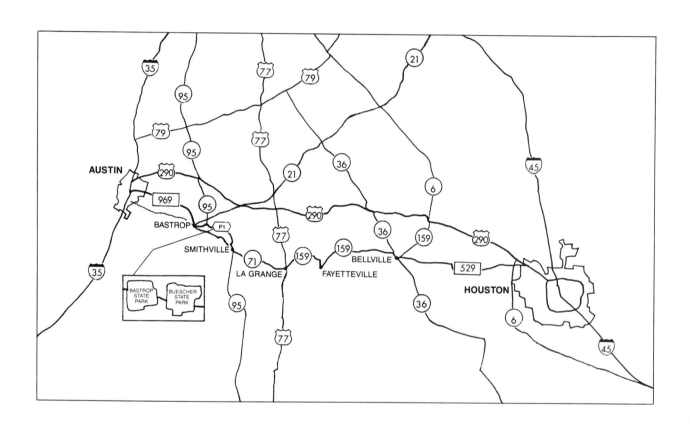

Houston to Austin

ROUTE
Any street through Houston to
  FM 529 - 25.0 miles
FM 520 west to Bellville - 32.0
  miles
TX 159 west to LaGrange -
  45.0 miles
TX 71 west - 22.5 miles
FM 153 to Buescher State Park -
  1.0 mile
Park Rd P1 north to Bastrop
  State Park - 13.0 miles
TX 21/Loop 150 west - 3.0 miles
TX 71 west - .8 miles
FM 969 west to Austin - 26.0
  miles

DISTANCE
168.30 miles/269.3 kilometers

TERRAIN
Flat, east of the Brazos River;
  gently rolling to rolling;
  west of the Brazos River.

TRAFFIC
Unbearable in Harris County.
Mostly nil to light elsewhere

There is nothing good to say about cycling in Houston. Any number of streets will take you to northeast Houston and connect with FM 529. Be extra careful and good luck!

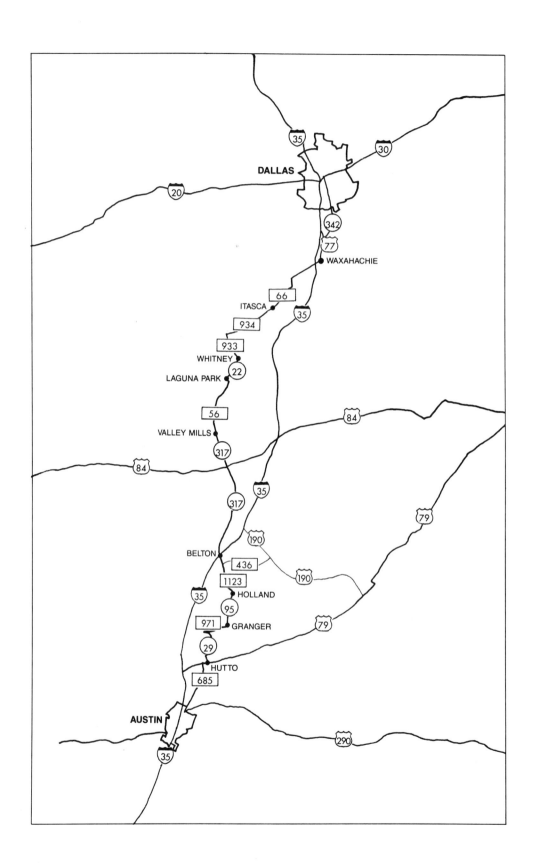

Austin to Dallas

TRAFFIC
Mostly light to nil. Traffic will
increase around Belton
and north of Waxahachie.

ROUTE
Dessau Rd north - 11.0 miles
FM 685 north- 7.8 miles
US 79 east to Hutto - 1.0 mile
FM 1660 north to Jonah - 7.3
  miles
TX 29 east - .1 mile
CO north - 4.7 miles
FM 971 east to Granger - 7.5
  miles
TX 95 north to Holland - 11.6
  miles
FM 1123 north - 12.8 miles
FM 436 west to Belton - 3.4
  miles
TX 317 north to Valley
  Mills - 47.0 miles
FM 56 north to Laguna
  Park - 18.0 miles
TX 22 east to Whitney - 8.5
  miles
FM 933 north - 10.0 miles
FM 934 east to Itasca - 16.0 miles
FM 66 east to Waxahachie -
  26.0 miles
US 77 north - 7.1 miles
TX 342 north to Dallas - 22.0
  miles

DISTANCE
221.8 miles/354.9 kilometers

TERRAIN
Gently rolling to flat, some
rolling between Valley Mills
and Whitney.

There are two sections on this route that are not on the state map. The first is from in-town Austin to FM 635 near Pflugerville. The route picks up Dessau Road in northeast Austin. Follow Dessau Road north for about 5.5 miles. The road will have a 90 degree turn to the left. Just *before* this turn is a road that leads right. A sign at the junction points the way to the Moose Lodge. Turn right here, and you will pass the lodge on the left. Next is a series of 90 degree turns. The main road is obvious, but the sequence is as follows: left turn, then right turn, and finally, another left turn. This whole series occurs in about a mile. From here, the road goes straight, crosses FM 1825, and connects with FM 635.

The second section is from Hutto to FM 971. In the center of Hutto are signs that show FM 1660 north. Turn left and follow FM 1660 to Jonah and the junction with TX 29. Turn right onto TX 29. About .1 (one-tenth) of a mile on TX 29 a small county road leads to the left. Turn left and go 1.5 miles to the first right turn. Go right here for .3 miles to a "T" junction. Turn left for 1.2 miles to another "T" junction. Here is a right-then-left dog-leg. This last left will take you to FM 971. Turn right on FM 971 to Granger. This section is harder to read about than it is to ride.

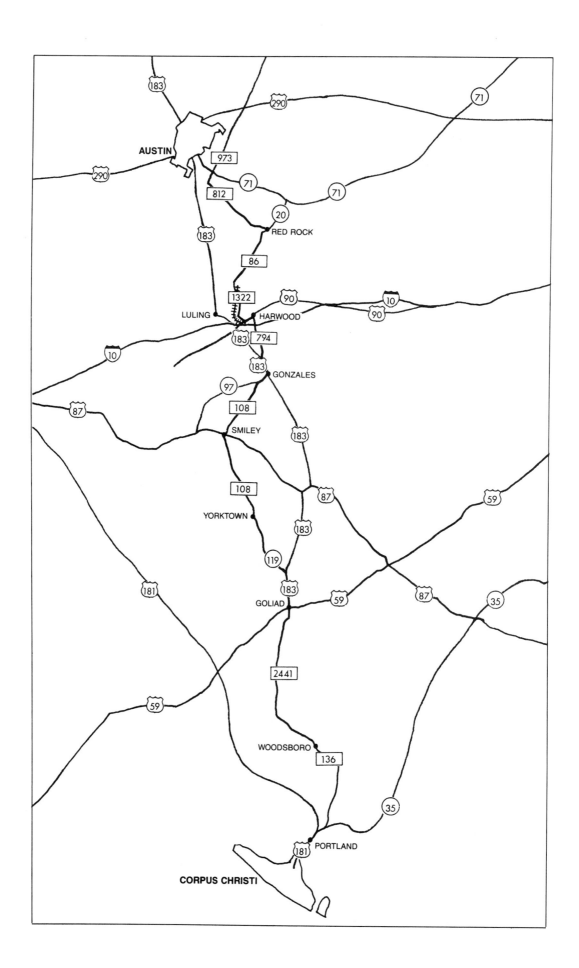

Austin to Corpus Christi

ROUTE
(OUT OF AUSTIN)
Pleasant Valley Road south
Riverside Drive East
Montopolis Drive South
Burleson Road east - 7.0 miles
FM 973 south - 1.6 miles
FM 812 east - 19.2 miles
TX 20 south - 1.8 miles
FM 86 south - 15.1 miles
FM 1322 south - 6.6 miles
Harwood Road east - 4.4 miles
US 90 east to Harwood - 1.5 miles
FM 794 south to Gonzales - 11.0 miles
US 183 south - 3.0 miles
TX 97 west - 3.5 miles
FM 108 south - 36.0 miles
TX 119 south - 19.2 miles
US 183 south - 12.0 miles
FM 2441 south to Woodsboro - 31.0 miles
FM 136 east - 30.0 miles
TX 35 west to Portland - 3.0 miles
US 181 south to Corpus Christi - 11.0 miles

DISTANCE
216.9 miles/347.1 kilometers

TERRAIN
Mostly gently rolling to flat

TRAFFIC
Mostly nil to light

Cycling south through McMahon on FM 86 the route will pass Daniels Chapel. Four miles farther is the junction with FM 1322. Turn left here. Five miles farther is the junction with FM 1386. Continue straight on FM 1322 for 1.5 miles more. The next left turn after the junction is a small paved lane. Turn left, and follow it to US 90. The last part of this road is unpaved and rough, but it is short. There is also a short, steep hill in this unpaved section. At the junction with US 90, turn left.

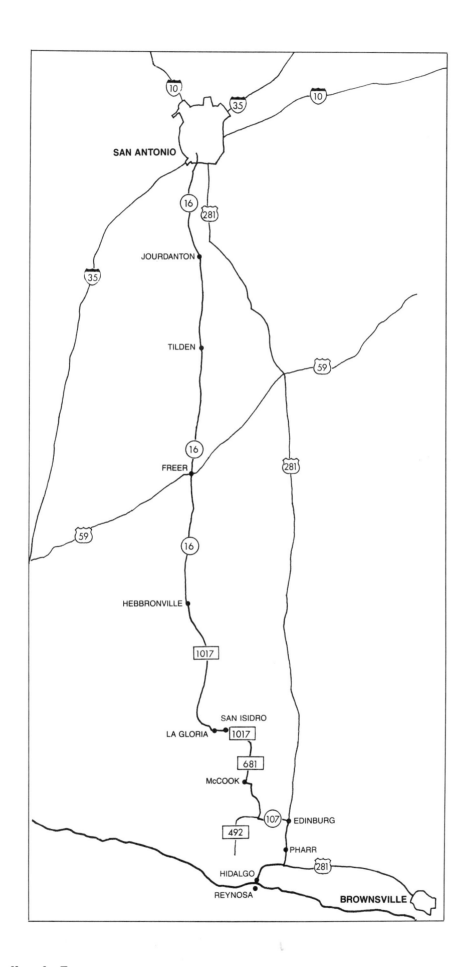

San Antonio to Rio Grande Valley

ROUTE
TX 16 south to Hebbronville -
148.0 miles
TX 285 east - 1.4 miles
FM 1017 south - 60.0 miles
FM 681 south - 27.0 miles
FM 490 east - 2.0 miles
TX 107 east to Edinburg - 9.0
miles
FM 681 south - 13.0 miles
US 281 south - 15.0 miles
US 281 east to Brownsville -
50.0 miles

DISTANCE
325.4 miles/520.6 kilometers

TERRAIN
Mostly flat, some gently
rolling

TRAFFIC
From south of Loop 1604 in
San Antonio to Edinburg,
virtually nil. On US 281
south, moderate. On US
281 east, light.

Caution! Do not attempt this route unless you are a seasoned cycle tourist. There are four deserted sections as follows: Jourdonton to Tilden, TX 16, 32 miles; Tilden to Freer, TX 16, 41 miles; Freer to Hebbronville, TX 16, 39 miles; Hebbronville to La Gloria, FM 1017, 48 miles, plus 5 more miles to San Isidro for a cafe. These sections have no water between them except at stock tanks. Water from stock tanks requires a First Need® water filtration system or equivalent. There is also little or no shade, and it can be an hour or more between passing cars from either direction. Frequent, strong headwinds, scorching sun, and little shade make this a potentially dangerous ride. Proper preparation, good conditioning, and lots of common sense will make this a safe, challenging ride.

Appendix: Sources of Information

Chambers of Commerce

Austin

901 W. Riverside Dr.
P.O. Box 1967, 78767
(512) 478-9383

Brownsville

1600 E. Elizabeth St.
P.O. Box 752, 78520
(512) 542-4341

Burnet

703 W. Buchanan Dr.
P.O. Box M, 78611
(512) 756-4267

Canyon

308 17th St.
P.O. Box 8, 79015
(806) 655-1183

Corpus Christi

1201 N. Shoreline
P.O. Box 640, 78403
(512) 882-6161

Kerrville

1200 Sidney Baker (Hwy 16)
P.O. Box 790, 78028
(512) 896-1155

Kountze

P.O. Box 878, 77625
(713) 246-2761

Leakey (Frio Canyon)

P.O. Box 743, 78873
(512) 232-6757

Nacogdoches

1801 North St.
P.O. Drawer 1918, 75963
(409) 564-7351

Navasota

117 S. La Salle
P.O. Box 530, 77868
(409) 825-6600

San Antonio

602 E. Commerce
P.O. Box 1628, 78296
(512) 229-2100

Spur

Has no chamber of
commerce.

Dallas

1507 Pacific, 75201
(214) 954-1111

Fort Davis

P.O. Box 378, 79734

Fredericksburg

101 N. Pioneer Plaza
P.O. Box 506, 78624
(512) 997-3444

Glen Rose

P.O. Box 605, 76043
(817) 897-2286

Houston

1100 Milam Bldg.
25th Floor, 77002
(713) 651-1313

Jefferson

116 W. Austin, 75657
(214) 665-2672

Other chamber of commerce addresses can be found in: *Johnson's Worldwide Chamber of Commerce Directory* in the business section of your public library. Copies of the book are available from

Johnson Publ. Co., Inc.
P.O. Box 455
8th and Van Buren
Loveland, CO 80537

Map Sources

City maps are usually available from the chambers of commerce. To get the Official Highway Travel Map write:

State Department of Highways and Public Transportation
P.O. Box 5064
Austin, TX 78763

The Texas County Highway Maps are available from the following address.

State Department of Highways & Public Transportation
P.O. Box 5064
Austin, TX 78763

The small fee is worth a detailed map that will supply you with dozens of bicycle tours of your own making. Most farm roads away from large cities are well maintained and usually have little traffic, making them perfect for the adventuresome cyclist. The county maps come in three scale sizes:

1. Quarter-scale (1 in. = 4 miles)—Each sheet measures 10″ × 14″. The maps are available in a bound single volume ($20) or as separate sheets (35¢). This size is the most convenient for carrying on your bike.

2. Half-scale (1 in. = 2 miles)—Each sheet measures 18″ × 25″. These are the best maps for planning your trip at home because the maps are large enough to read without straining and economical enough to afford. Each map is 50¢.

3. Full-scale (1 in. = 1 mile)—Each sheet is huge and costs $2. this is the easiest sheet to read, but very unwieldy. If you have plenty of storage space and a large table to lay them out on, then go for them.

Request an order form from the highway department that lists all the county and supplemental maps or ask specifically for the maps desired and enclose a money order or check.

Bicycle Shops

Only three shops are located in tour areas other than those found in major metropolitan centers.

Amarillo (Panhandle/Canyon)

Mason's Pro Frame Shop
3333-C Coulter Dr., 79121
(806) 359-3826
Erin Mason, owner/manager

Kerrville (Hill Country)

Bicycles, Etc.
233 Earl Garrett, 78028
(512) 896-6864
Dick Mauldin, owner/manager

Nacogdoches (East Texas)

The Cyclesmith
247 E. College, 75961
(409) 564-0385
Chris Roach, manager

INDEX

A. B. McGill and Co. General Store, 49
Adolphus Sterne Home, 18
Alley, Dan N. and Victoria, 28
Amaladeras Creek, 22
Amarillo, 67
Anderson, 9–12
Anderson Courthouse, 11
"Angel Marker," 18
Angelina National Forest, 24
Appomattox, 11
Architectural Digest, 22
Armadillos, 47
Atchison, Topeka and Santa Fe, 58
Attoyac, 22
Austin, 85, 87, 89

Baines, George W., 13
Bank of San Augustine, 24
Bank sundial, 24
Barrington, home of Anson Jones, 7
Barrow, Clyde, 9
Bay Food Store, 9
Bayou Loco, 20
Beaumont, 55
Bertram, 49
Bethel Church, 47
Bicycles, Etc., 33, 36
Big Cypress Bayou, 30
Big Thicket, 55, 58
Birds, marsh, 72
Birds, migratory, 72
Bison, 14, 75
Bloys Camp Meeting, 76
Blue Mountain, 76
"Bluebonnet Capital of Texas," 46
Blum, 62
Bragg, 58
Brazos Point, 62
Brazos River, 3, 7, 13–14, 59, 62–63
Brooks-Ward House, 6
Brownsville, 78
Brushy Butte, 69
Buffalo Lake National Wildlife Refuge, 70
Buffington House, 11
Burnet, 44, 46, 50–51
Burnet Cemetery, 46
Burnet County Heritage Society, 44
Burnet County Historical Commission, 44
Burnet County Historical Society, 44
Burnet County Jail, 44, 46

Caddell, Julie, 9
Caddo Lake State Park, 25, 30
Camels, 39
Camp Verde Store, 39
Canyon, 67, 69–70, 72
Capitol Peak, 69
Caprock Escarpment, 64
"The Castle", Templeman-Grice House, 6

Center Point, 39
Charles Schreiner Mansion, 33, 36
Childress, George C., 14
Chireno, 22, 23
City Cafe, 6
Civilian Conservation Corps, 44
Clark, William S., 18
Collins House, 28
Continental Motel, 15
Corpus Christi, 89
The Cottage, 28
Cow Creek, 49
Cowboy Artists of America Museum, 36
Cowboy Camp, 76
Craig House, 6
Croton Breaks, 64
Cushing, 19
Cypress Creek, 39

Dallas, 83, 87
Dance Brothers, 11
Daniels Chapel, 89
Davis Mountains, 73
Davis Mountains State Park, 75–76
Deer, mule and whitetail, 37, 40, 47, 49, 76
Del Norte Inn, 33
Devil's Tombstone, 69
Doe Run Creek, 7
Douglass, 20–21
Dry Creek, 49

Easter Hill Country Tour, 36, 43
Egypt, 39
Emory Terrell House, 6
Etoile, 24
Excelsior House, 25

Falkenbury, Mrs. T. S., 3
Fantrop Inn, 9
Fara's International, 33
Field Store Community, 14
First Need ®, 91
First Presbyterian Church, Navasota, 6
Flat Rock Lake, 33
Fort Croghan, 44, 46
Fort Croghan Museum, 44
Fort Davis, 73
Fort Davis National Historic Site, 73, 75–76
Foster, R. B. S., 9
Foster Gin, 9
Fredericksburg, 33, 36, 40, 42
Fredericksburg Self-Guiding Auto Tour, 37, 42
Fredonia Inn, 15, 19–20
Freer, 9
Frio River, 79

Garner State Park, 78
Giesel House, 3
Gil Y'Barbo, 15
Glen Rose, 59, 62–63
Granger, 87
Grassy Creek Mobile Home Park, 3

Great Panic of 1870, 11
Greenwood General Merchandise, 13
Grimes County, 8–9
Grimes County Historical Commission, 9
Guadalupe River, 38–39

Hale House, 25
Hall, 29
Ham Creek Park, 62
Hamilton Creek, 50–51
Hammett Motel, 3
Hardin County Courthouse, 55
Harper, 40–41
Hebbronville, 91
Hickey Branch,
Highland Lakes, 48, 50
Hill Country Museum, 33
"Historic Grimes County and Anderson, Texas," 9
Holiday Inn, 15
Holland Creek, 9
Holland, Frances, 9
Holland, Tapley, 9
Honey Creek, 49
Honey Island, 55
Houston, 83, 85
Houston, Gen. Sam, 11, 18, 22
Hoya, Charles, 18
Hoya Land Office, 18
Hoya Memorial Library and Museum, 18–19
Hubbard, Joan, 42
Huff-N-Puff, 31, 51
Hutto, 87

Independence Hall, 7
Indian Lodge, 75
Indian Mound Oak, 18
Inks Lake State Park, 44

Jackrabbits, 47
Jeff Davis County Courthouse, 75
Jefferson, 22, 25, 30–32
Jefferson Historic District, 28
Jesse Youens House, 6
Johnson, Lyndon B., 12–13
Jordan, Ruthmary, 25
Jourdonton, 9

Karnack, 25
Kellyville, 31
Kerrville, 33, 36, 40–41
Kerrville Convention and Visitors' Bureau, 33
Kerrville State Park, 33, 36
Kerrville Winter Music Festival, 36
Kitchens Creek, 30
Kountry Kupboard Gift Shop and Restaurant, 7
Kountze, 55
Kountze Fire Tower, 58

La Calle del Norte, 18
La Gloria, 91
Lake Marble Falls, 50

Lake Nacogdoches, 21
Lake O'The Pines,
Lake Sam Rayburn, 24
Lake Victor, 47
Lake Waxahachie, 83
Lake Whitney, 62
Lake Whitney Recreational Area, 62
Lanana Bayou, 22
"The Land of Milk and Honey," 9
La Salle, René Robert, 3, 7
Las Piedras, Col. Jose de, 15
Leakey, 78
Leonard, Linda and Mark, 25
Limpia Canyon, 75
Limpia Creek, 75
Limpia Hotel, 73
Little Bayou Loco, 20
Little Cypress Bayou, 31
Lodi, 29–30
Longhorn Caverns State Park, 44, 48
Looneyville, 20
Lost Maples State Park, 78–79
Love's Store, 39
Lucas Home, 6

McDonald Creek, 64
McDonald Observatory, 75
McMahon, 89
Madera Canyon, 76
Magnolia, 13–14
The Magnolias, 28
Main Street Walking Tour, 3
Marble Falls, 51
Martinsville, 22
Masonic Lodge, Burnet, 46
Mauldin, Dick and Sarah, 33, 36
Melrose, 23
Methodist Church, Plantersville, 13
Mill Creek, 29
Millard's Crossing, 18
Millican, Andrew, 8
Millican, town of, 8
Missionary Baptists, 18
Moose Lodge, 87
Morman Mill, 50
Mount Blanc Church, 50–51
Mount Livermore, 76
Mount Locke, 75
Mount Maria Church, 29
Mount Tiuy, 38
The Museum of Natural History of the
   Davis Mountains, 75

Nacogdoches, 14, 20–22, 24
Nacogdoches High School, 18–19
Nacogdoches Indian Village, 18
Nance, Chuck and John, 25
Nance's Boat Tours, 25
Nasonite Indian Village, 18
Navasota, 3–8, 11–14
Navasota Chamber of Commerce, 3, 9
Navasota River, 7, 13
Neal, George D., home of, 6
The Neill Museum, 76
Nemo, 63
New Jefferson Inn, 25
"The Notch," 51

Oak Grove Cemetery, 18–19
Oatmeal Creek, 49
Oil, first discovery of, 22
Old Midway Inn, 22
Old Nacogdoches University Building,
   18–19
Old North Church, 18–19
Old Stone Fort, 14–17
Olive Branch, 49
Orten Hill, 21–24
Overland Trail Museum, 75

P. A. Smith Hotel, 3
Palo Duro Canyon State Park, 67
Pampell's Pharmacy, 33, 36
Pedernales River, 41
Pflugerville, 87
Piedmont Hotel, 10
Piedmont Springs Resort, 10
Pioneer Museum, 40
Plantersville, 13–14
Plantersville Baptist Church, 13
Plantersville Masonic Lodge, 13
Point of Rocks, 76
"Powder House," 44
Pride House, 25
Pronghorn Antelope, 76
Prude House, 75

Radke's Deer Processing, 42
Remington, Frederic, 36
Retreat Community, 14
Ried's Prairie First Baptist Church, 14
Rio Grande Valley, 91
Rio Vista, 62
Riverboats, 22, 31
Road Runners, 47, 49
Roan's Prairie, 12
Roan's Prairie Baptist Church, 12
Roberts, John S., 18
The Rockpile, 76
Rocky Creek, 10
Roland Jones House, 20
Rulfs, Dietrich, 19–20
Rusk, Thomas J., 18–19
Russell, Charles, 36
Russell Fork of the San Gabriel River,
   49

Sabinal River, 79
Saint Hollands Church, 14
San Antonio, 91
San Augustine, 22–23
San Gabriel River, Russell Fork of, 49
San Isidro, 91
Sand Hill, 23
Sand Hill School, 23
Saratoga, 58
Savannah Church, 29
Sawtooth Mountain, 76
Scenic Loop, 75
Segno, 58
Shady Grove, 21, 49

Shady Grove Church and Cemetery,
   21, 49
Sherry Inn Motel, 25
Skillman Grove, 76
Skyline Drive, 76
Soldier Mound, 64
Spain, Eastern Provinces of,
   government seat, 15
Spring Creek, 40
Spur, 64, 66
Steele House, 6
Stephen F. Austin State University,
   18–20
Stewart-Davis House, 6
Stone House, 15
Swift, 22

Taylor, Charles S., 18
Templeman-Grice House, "The Castle,"
   6
Ten Mile Creek, 8
Tenaha, 24
Texas, Republic of, 18–19
Texas Declaration of Independence, 7,
   14, 18–19
Texas Hills Sporting Range, 41
Texas Renaissance Festival, 14
Texas Revolution, 18
Texas State Arts and Crafts Fair, 36
Third Creek, 38
Tierra Linda Ranch, 41
Tilden, 91
Tivy, James, 38
Tivydale Community, 41
Trailer Village Camper Park, 15
Travis, Col. William B., 9, 22
Trinity Church, 30
Turkeys, 43, 47
Turning Basin, 31
Turtle Creek, 37

Umbarger, 70
Utopia, 79

Van der Hoya, Joseph, 18
Vanderpool, 79
Vanguard Inn, 3
Verde Creek, 39
Votaw, 58

Wallace Park Unit, Texas Department of
   Corrections, 14
Waltrip Ranch, 11
Washington-on-the-Brazos State Park,
   7–8
Waxahachie, 83
Waxahachie Creek, 83
White River, 64
White River Dam, 66
Whoop-De-Do, 62, 66
Willow City, 42
Wise Manor, 28

Zion Hills First Baptist Church, 19